=

Ac

Working Papers in Doctrine

Working Papers in Doctrine

MAURICE WILES

SCM PRESS LTD

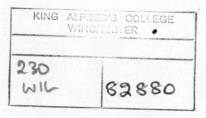
334 01807 2

First published 1976
by SCM Press Ltd
56 Bloomsbury Street, London
© SCM Press Ltd 1976

Printed in Great Britain by
Western Printing Services Ltd
Bristol

CONTENTS

PREFACE

Some reviewers have described my book *The Remaking of Christian Doctrine* as a small work in which to put forward so radical a thesis. Such comments are not without justification, though I only half apologise for the fault. The shorter form may enable the central issues to stand out more clearly. It is then possible to expand or to defend them at the points at which such expansion or defence proves to be most needed.

One issue where such further substantiation seems to be called for is the critical attitude adopted towards many of the traditional formulations of doctrine. This is something that has arisen out of my specifically historical work, particularly in the formative patristic period. Some of that more detailed historical study is incorporated in my earlier book, *The Making of Christian Doctrine*, but it has primarily found expression in articles on particular issues in various theological journals. It is for this reason that I have brought together a number of those articles to form this book. (Details of the original publication of each article are given in the notes at the end pp. 194 ff.) They have been selected with the aim of showing how my attitude to doctrinal tradition springs out of historical study of that tradition. The articles fall into two groups, with a transitional paper in the middle.

The first group (written between 1957 and 1967) deals directly with problems in the history of early Christian doctrine. Most of the papers do none the less give some brief indication of the possible significance of the historical investigation for contemporary theological work. But the treatment of the issues in the papers themselves is straightforwardly historical and has not,

I hope, been distorted in any way with a view to supporting any contemporary theological thesis.

The transitional paper was the outcome of an invitation to contribute to a consultation of Lutheran and Anglican scholars. The somewhat longer style of title bears witness to the fact that the precise subject of the paper was one formulated not by me but by the organizers of that consultation. But it deals in general terms with the subject that is central to all these papers – the authority of the church's early doctrinal tradition for the church today.

The second group of papers (written between 1968 and 1973) is concerned with the appropriate method of work for Christian doctrine today. But all of them embody as an important aspect of that concern reflection on the early doctrinal tradition and its significance for the contemporary theologian's work. This is partly for personal reasons. As one who has spent much of his working life studying and teaching patristic doctrine it is for me the most natural approach to questions of doctrine. But I also believe it to be a necessary element in any satisfactory approach to Christian doctrine, because of the all-pervasive influence that the patristic formulation of doctrine has had on the whole subsequent history of Christian thought.

The papers are thus held together by a common concern. I hope their publication will be of help to those who are puzzled why I should feel the need for a 'remaking' process in the work of Christian doctrine. The fact that the papers have such a common concern means that there is a certain amount of overlap between them. In general I think that such overlap as there is helps to build up the cumulative and developing case that the papers as a whole are designed to illustrate. The very occasional repetition of the same specific point has been unavoidable with papers brought together from different sources and reproduced in their original form.

Attitude to past tradition is not of course the only issue that has arisen in discussion of *The Remaking of Christian Doctrine*. In that book, for example, I was primarily concerned to lay bare what seemed to me to be the framework appropriate to a contemporary scheme of doctrine. There is clearly more that needs to be said about how that framework is to be filled in. In particular how is the place of Jesus in Christianity to be understood? If one finds the kind of difficulty that I have suggested in incarnational accounts, what place does Jesus hold and how ought Christians to think and speak of him? These and other more substantive issues I hope to be able to develop more fully in a later book.

I

Some Reflections on the Origins of the Doctrine of the Trinity

'The doctrine of the Trinity is the product of rational reflection on those particular manifestations of the divine activity which centre in the birth, ministry, crucifixion, resurrection and ascension of Jesus Christ and the gift of the Holy Spirit to the Church ... it could not have been discovered without the occurrence of those events, which drove human reason to see that they required a trinitarian God for their cause.' This statement of Dr Hodgson about the source of the doctrine of the Trinity would, I imagine, be accorded widespread assent today, together with its negative corollary that it is a fair criticism of particular theologies of the Trinity to say that their thought is based on 'the acceptance of the Bible as giving revelation in the form of propositions concerning the inner mysteries of the Godhead'.[2] Dr Hodgson's approach, it is generally assumed, will still provide us with an essential rather than an economic doctrine of the Trinity. The purpose of this article is to question whether the full implications of his approach to this subject have been recognized.

Dr Bethune-Baker asserts that 'Sabellianism, in recognizing only a Trinity in human experience, disregards the fact that such a Trinity of revelation is only possible if the very being of the Godhead, which is thus revealed, is itself a Trinity'.[3] The validity of this assertion does not need to come up for question here. But, on Dr Hodgson's thesis, the corollary of this must also be true. There can be no knowledge of an essential Trinity, except through a Trinity of revelation. Do we, in fact, find such an unmistakable Trinity of revelation in God's dealings with mankind?

The most obvious distinction to which the concept of God's self-revelation gives rise is the distinction between God in himself and God active in the world, accommodating himself to the needs of men. This was a distinction which both Greek thought and post-exilic Jewish thought about God naturally suggested at the outset of the Christian era. It did, in fact, play its part in determining the ascription of particular acts of God to particular persons of the Trinity. Thus Irenaeus writes:

> It was not the Father of all, who is not seen by the world, the Maker of all who said 'Heaven is my throne, and earth is my footstool: what house will ye build me or what is the place of my rest?' and who 'comprehendeth the earth with his hand and with his span the heaven' – it was not He that came and stood in a very small space and spake with Abraham; but the Word of God, who was ever with mankind, and made known beforehand what should come to pass in the future, and taught men the things of God.[4]

The same argument in relation to the anthropomorphisms of the Old Testament is developed more fully by Novatian. God is infinite and contains all things; yet the scripture speaks of God descending to the tower of Babel. The selfsame author within Scripture declares on the one hand that 'no man can see God and live' and on the other that 'God was seen of Abraham'. From these apparent contradictions he concludes: 'So it may be understood that it was not the Father who was seen . . . but the Son who has both been accustomed to descend and to be seen because He has descended.'[5] Tertullian applies the same argument to the text of the New Testament. St John declares emphatically that 'no man hath seen God at any time', and yet the same writer testifies that he and his fellow apostles had both seen and handled Christ. So he concludes: 'The Father acts by mind and thought, whilst the Son, who is in the Father's mind and thought, gives form to what he sees.'[6] But this line of

argument would have led to a binitarian rather than to a trinitarian form of theology, as is clearly shown by the conclusion of
the passage quoted from Irenaeus: 'So then the Father is God
and the Son is God; for that which is begotten of God is God.'[7]
In the Christian doctrine of the Trinity all three persons are
involved both in the eternal and essential life of God and also
in his activity and self-revelation to the world. Our Trinity of
revelation must therefore be sought not in a distinction between
God in himself and God active, but in the threefold character
of the activity of God in the world.

As we come to this stage in our investigation, it is important to
remember just what it is that we are doing. We are not starting
with the assumption of a revealed trinitarian doctrine of God
and then looking at the manner of God's self-revealing activity
in the world to see if it can appropriately be understood in a way
which corresponds to the already known trinitarian nature of
God. We are, on the contrary, seeking to look at the activity
of God to see if it is of such unquestionably threefold character
that we are forced, in order to explain it rationally, to postulate a
threefold character in God himself. The Anglican Catechism
certainly suggests that there is such a threefold activity, when it
speaks of 'God the Father, who made me and all the world, God
the Son, who hath redeemed me and all mankind and God the
Holy Ghost, who sanctifieth me and all the elect people of God.'
This, it should be noted, is not really one but a combination of
two different threefold analyses of the activity of God. The first
is a division based on the type of activity-creation, redemption
and sanctification being ascribed respectively to Father, Son, and
Holy Ghost. The second is a division based on the range of
activity – all creation, rational life, spiritual life. Does either or
both of these represent such a threefold division of revelation as
we are looking for? At first sight it might appear that they do.
But when we consider them more carefully it is not at all clear
that they do correspond to the divisions of the Trinity. Thus
while the first division – creation, redemption, sanctification – is
probably the one that springs most naturally to the modern mind,

it is doubtful whether it is to be found at all in the New Testament or in the earliest period, when trinitarian doctrine was first
being worked out. The New Testament most explicitly asso-
ciates the second person of the Trinity with the work of creation,[8]
and this concept of the creative activity of the Logos is a dominant theme throughout the early patristic period. The second
division – that by range of activity – has at least one exact
counterpart in the earliest period. According to Origen, the
Father is concerned with all life, the Son with all rational beings,
and the Holy Spirit with specifically Christian life.[9] But this
is not an unvarying or generally accepted principle. Rufinus
'corrects' the theology of Origen in the passage just quoted so as
to make it more in accord with the normal view by classing
Father and Son together as equally concerned with the whole
range of creation. Nor is the restriction of the Spirit to spiritual
life in the narrower sense of the words one that is consistently
maintained. Irenaeus and others regularly associate the Spirit
with the work of creation.[10] It is evident from the general tenor
of fourth-century teaching that the description of the Spirit as
life-giver in the Constantinopolitan creed was not intended to
be understood in any restricted sense.[11] It seems absurd to claim
that we are aware of the trinitarian nature of God through the
threefold character of revelation, and at the same time to maintain that that threefold character of revelation does not precisely
correspond to the three persons of the Trinity. Yet this dilemma
faces us whatever threefold division we choose to make. God
has revealed himself in three stages – Old Testament dispensation, the incarnation, New Testament dispensation; but if we
try to fit this division to the persons of the Trinity, we find that
it fits some of the facts (e.g. John 7.39: 'The Spirit was not yet
given because Jesus was not yet glorified') but not others (e.g.
'who spake by the prophets'),[12] and this particular division has
been rightly seen to lead to dangerous heresy.

In his essay 'On the evolution of the Doctrine of the Trinity',[13]
Dr Kirk sees the problem in very much the same terms as it is
posed in this article. He believes that the required differentia in

experience can be found in three different kinds of relationship which exist between God and man. There is the 'King-servant' relation which points to the Father, a relation of personal 'communion' which points to the Son, and a relation which is still personal but to which he gives the name 'possession', which points to the Spirit. This is certainly an acute and suggestive analysis, but it is questionable whether it fulfils all that is required of it. Dr Kirk claims that these 'three modes of intercourse . . . point to three distinguishable termini within the Godhead, of each of which hypostatic character must, and can, be predicated without impairing the divine unity'.[14] But he produces very little evidence to substantiate the claim and has to admit that the differentia is by no means absolute. 'It would be impossible', he writes, 'to analyse the New Testament or the Fathers and show that all the passages which refer to this kind of divine action [sc. possession] are associated with the Spirit, and none of them with the name of the Son.'[15] But such an analysis is surely required if his case is to be accepted, and I do not believe that it could be made.

The impossibility of finding such a clear-cut threefold division of activity is perhaps most clearly shown by the uncertainty throughout the early period as to what activities in many of the primary spheres of God's self-revelation ought to be attributed to the Son and what to the Spirit. This can be illustrated from the spheres of incarnation, inspiration, and creation.

Luke 1.35 had declared explicitly that the conception of Christ was effected by the coming of Holy Spirit upon the Virgin Mary. Later orthodoxy, as expressed in the Apostles' creed, has therefore attributed this crucial act, by which the incarnation was effected, to the third person of the Trinity. The majority of early writers, however, were led by the logic of their thought to identify Holy Spirit in this context with the Logos, and so to attribute the conception to the second person of the Trinity. This is done explicitly by Justin and Tertullian.[16] Other writers are less explicit in the identification of Spirit and Logos in their treatment of the passage, but their language seems

normally to imply the same interpretation.[17] Irenaeus' view of
the matter is particularly difficult to determine with clarity but
according to the considered judgment of J. Armitage Robinson,
'he seems to prefer to think of a co-operation of the Word of God
and the Wisdom of God – the two Hands of God to whom the
creation of the first-formed man was due'.[18] This general uncertainty about the efficient agent in the work of incarnation is
paralleled by an uncertainty about the efficient agent of consecra-
tion in the Eucharist to whom the prayer of Epiklesis should be
addressed.[19]

Both scripture and the Nicene creed have accustomed us to
think of the inspiration of the Old Testament prophets as the
particular function of the Holy Spirit. This indeed represents
also the general mind of the early Fathers. In fact Justin and
Irenaeus even speak in such a way as to imply that the inspiration
of the prophets was the primary and distinctive characteristic of
the Spirit. Thus Justin speaks of worshipping the Father, the
Son, and the prophetic Spirit,[20] and of the use in baptism of the
name of the Father Lord God of the universe, and of Jesus
Christ, who was crucified under Pontius Pilate, and of the Holy
Spirit, who through the prophets announced the things relating
to Jesus.[21] And Irenaeus says that heretics either 'despise the
Father, or do not accept the Son, that is speak against the dispensation of His incarnation, or do not accept the Spirit, that is,
reject prophecy',[22] and in a positive exposition of the faith of the
apostles he speaks of belief in 'one God the Father almighty,
Who made the heaven and the earth and the seas and all the
things in them; and in one Christ Jesus, the Son of God, who
was made flesh for our salvation, and in the Holy Spirit, Who
through the prophets proclaimed the saving dispensations . . .'[23]
Yet to many of the early writers (including Justin and Irenaeus)
it seemed reasonable to associate this work of inspiration also with
the divine Logos. Thus Justin, in developing the argument from
prophecy in the *First Apology*, attributes the utterances of the
prophets to 'the prophetic spirit' and to 'the Holy Spirit of
prophecy', and yet in the selfsame passage declares the prophets

to be 'inspired by the divine word who moves them'.[24] Irenaeus in a single chapter of the *Adversus Haereses* speaks first of the prophets 'receiving their prophetic gift from the Word' and of 'the Word of God foretelling from the beginning that God should be seen by men', and a little later on of the same prophets as acting 'according to the suggestions of the Spirit' and of 'the Spirit of God as pointing out things to come by them'.[25] Similarly Hippolytus writes: 'One God gave the law and the prophets; and in giving them, He made them speak by the Holy Ghost, in order that being gifted with the inspiration of the Father's power, they might declare the Father's counsel and will. Acting then in these prophets, the Word spoke of Himself. For already He became His own herald.'[26] Thus none of these writers finds any incongruity in ascribing the work of inspiration both to the Holy Spirit and the Logos. In fact Lietzmann declares of Justin that, 'according to his theory, the Son, as the Logos, is identical with the Spirit which revealed itself in the prophets',[27] Swete states that Clement of Alexandria 'connects the Word and the Spirit, when he speaks of the inspiration of the prophets, ascribing this to either Person almost indiscriminately';[28] and Lawson asserts that for Irenaeus the Son and the Spirit are 'equal and interchangeable in function', explicitly in the matter of inspiration and implicitly in the matter of revelation.[29] This last judgment requires some slight qualification in view of the fact that Irenaeus once again seems to think of the inspiration of Scripture as the joint activity of the Word and the Spirit,[30] and even attempts to draw a distinction between their respective roles. The Word is the source of revelation about himself, the Spirit the agent. In revelation of the Father, the Word is also agent.[31] None the less, the conclusion is evident that the inspiration of Scripture is not an activity which points directly to or which can be associated exclusively with one particular person of the Trinity.

It is in the third selected sphere, that of the work of creation, that this uncertainty is most widespread. Modern thought is most inclined to attribute this kind of activity either directly to the

Father or in its more immanentist aspects to the Spirit. But the
early Fathers ascribe the work of creation either to the Logos
alone, or else to the Logos and the Spirit together. Eusebius
describes how the Logos by his divine prerogative

always continuously pervades the whole matter of the elements and of
actual bodies; and, as being creator-word of God, stamps on it the principles of the wisdom derived from Him. He impresses life on what is
lifeless and form on what is itself formless and indeterminate, reproducing
in the qualities of the bodies the values and the unembodied forms inherent in Him; He sets into an all-wise and all-harmonious motion things
that are on their own account lifeless and immobile – earth, water, air and
fire; He orders everything out of disorder, giving development and completion; with the actual power of deity and logos, He all but forces all
things; He pervades all things and grasps all things; yet contracts no injury
from any nor is sullied in Himself.[32]

More frequently, especially under the influence of Ps. 33.6, this
kind of thing is ascribed to the Son and the Spirit together. Thus
Athenagoras speaks of God 'framing all things by the Logos
and holding them in being by His Spirit'.[33] Irenaeus frequently
speaks in this kind of way. He speaks of God 'producing
creatures by His Word and fashioning everything by His
Spirit',[34] 'establishing all things by His word and binding them
together by His wisdom',[35] 'making things by His word and
adorning them by His wisdom',[36] or again of 'the Son executing
and fabricating', while 'the Spirit nourishes and increases'.[37]
Similarly Hippolytus says that 'God created all things by the
Logos and arranged them by the Wisdom'.[38] Dr Prestige defines
the distinction between the roles of the Logos and the Spirit here
as a 'connection of the universal scheme and fundamental principles of the creation, regarding creation not as a finished product
but as a continuous process, with the Logos, and that of its
living growth and progress with the Spirit of Life'.[39] Irenaeus
is the one early writer who makes a similar attempt to show that
the distinction is a logical and significant one. 'Since the word',
he says, 'establishes, that is to say, gives body and grants the

reality of being, and the Spirit gives order and form to the diversity of powers, rightly and fittingly is the Word called the Son, and the Spirit the Wisdom of God'.[40] No doubt some such distinction can be drawn, but it is hardly one that *requires* us to think of different persons within the Godhead. Nor, as we have seen, was it consistently maintained. Even Ps. 33.6 with its reference to 'word' and 'breath' was not always interpreted as implying the second and third persons of the Trinity. Tertullian interprets both parts of the verse as referring to the Word, so that, whereas the verse suggested to Irenaeus the picture of the Son and the Spirit as the two hands of God, for Tertullian the Word is in Himself both the hands of God.[41] All this kind of thinking is consciously based upon the concept of Wisdom to be found in the Old Testament. Its ascription to the second or third person of the Trinity therefore depended on whether Wisdom was to be identified with the Son or with the Spirit. Theophilus, in the earliest example of the word τρίας in this context, speaks of the 'triad, God and His Word and His Wisdom'.[42] Irenaeus also makes explicit identification of Wisdom and the Holy Spirit.[43] But the majority of writers, partly under the influence of 1 Cor. 1.24 and partly motivated by the obvious similarity of idea between Sophia and Logos, preferred to identify Wisdom with the second person of the Trinity.[44]

'Later theology,' wrote E. F. Scott, 'has been unable to define the threefold nature in such a way as to preserve a real distinction between the Spirit and Christ.'[45] And while this may be an overstatement when applied to the whole historical development of theology, it seems at least to be true of the ante-Nicene period. The thought of the earliest Fathers about God was not so unfailingly threefold in character that they were forced to think in trinitarian terms. Their thought about God was at least as much binitarian as trinitarian. Why, then, should Christian thought about God have taken so clear a trinitarian form, if its content was as much binitarian as trinitarian? The answer appears to be that the threefold form was a basic datum for Christian thought from the very beginning. If not emphasized, it was at least present in Scripture. From a comparatively early time it seems to have provided the framework for semi-credal confessions, summaries of the faith, and baptismal practice. We have seen that many of the writers of the first three centuries were far from clear about the distinctions between the three persons of the Godhead. Many of the passages in which they speak most clearly in a threefold trinitarian fashion about God are passages in which there are definite allusions to baptism or which read like stereotyped summaries of the faith along lines given in catechetical instruction. Thus Justin Martyr has an explicit reference to baptism in the trinitarian passage already quoted.[46] Irenaeus sums up his most explicitly trinitarian summary of the faith with the words: 'Therefore the baptism of our rebirth comes through these three articles, granting us rebirth unto God the Father, through His Son, by the Holy Spirit.'[47] Origen describes how 'when we come to the grace of baptism, renouncing all other gods and lords, we confess only God the Father and Son and Holy Spirit'.[48] Tertullian, in arguing for the distinct personality of the Son, refers to the dominical command to baptize into the Father and the Son and the Holy Ghost, and adds: 'For not once but thrice are we baptised into each several person at each several name.'[49] Origen uses a similar argument in support of the true dignity of the person of the Spirit.[50] Similarly, numerous examples could be given of expositions of 'the rule of faith', which fall into a clear trinitarian form. We have already quoted one such passage from Irenaeus.[51] Origen makes it quite clear that faith in God and Jesus Christ and the Holy Spirit is the heart of apostolic teaching.[52] Tertullian's summaries of the faith are not so clearly trinitarian in character, although they tend in that direction.[53] If these trinitarian forms were a later evolutionary development from an earlier universal practice of simple christological confessions or binitarian creeds, then they would have to be regarded more as a result than a cause of the adoption of a threefold scheme in thought about God. But this is not the case. In his *Early Christian Creeds* Dr Kelly has shown that this conception of the development of trinitarian credal forms was an unproved axiom of certain scholars. He has shown that the trinitarian pattern in stylized expressions of faith is present from the very beginning.[54] It is true that it is present alongside simpler christological and binitarian forms, but that is quite sufficient for the purposes of our argument. If trinitarian forms were in existence at all from the beginning, it is highly probable that they would exercise considerable effect upon later thought. It was easier for binitarian forms to be expanded, than for existing trinitarian forms to be truncated. Where argument, going beyond the simple appeal to established belief, is employed, the appeal is not so much to the threefold character of God's revelation as experienced but rather to the letter of Scripture. Thus Origen bases his clear distinction of the three persons constituting the one Trinity on the wording of the gospels in which Jesus speaks of the Father as ἄλλος from himself, and of the Spirit as ἄλλος παράκλητος.[55]

We are therefore bound to conclude that the ante-Nicene Fathers did not adopt a trinitarian scheme of thought about God because they found themselves compelled to do so as the only rational means of explanation of their experience of God in Christ. Rather they came to accept a trinitarian form, because it was the already accepted pattern of expression, even though they often found it difficult to interpret their experience of God in this particular threefold way.

By the fourth century, however, the issues at stake had changed. The threefold pattern was fully and firmly established. The main efforts of the catholic theologians were directed against the 'semi-Arian' tradition, with its radical division of the three hypostases within the Godhead, and the Macedonian tendency to deny the full divinity of the Spirit. For this purpose the difficulty of making any clear division between the three persons of the Trinity, which had been something of an embarrassment at the earlier stage of development, was a fact of incomparable value for the establishment and defence of orthodoxy. Time and again, in arguing for the identity of substance between the three persons of the Trinity, they base their case upon the identity of

their operations. This perhaps finds its clearest expression in the
words of Gregory of Nyssa:

If we recognise that the operation of the Father, the Son and the Holy
Spirit is one, with no point of difference or variation, then we are forced
to infer from the identity of their operation the unity of their natures.
Sanctification, life-giving illumination and consolation and all similar
gifts are the work alike of the Father, the Son and the Holy Spirit. And
no one should attribute the power of sanctification in the especial sense to
the Spirit, when he hears the Saviour in the Gospel saying to the Father
regarding the disciples: 'Father, sanctify them in Thy name'. So too all the
other gifts, which are produced in the lives of those deserving them, come
equally from the Father, the Son and the Holy Spirit. And the same is
true of every grace or virtue – guidance, life, consolation, translation to
immortality, passing into freedom – in fact it is true of any boon there
may be, which comes down to us. . . . Thus the identity of operation in
Father, Son and Holy Spirit shows clearly the indistinguishable character
of their nature.[56]

In one form or another, the same argument is repeated by all the
main writers of the fourth century.[57] The various gifts of God
are not the gifts of one particular member of the Trinity; every
gift comes from the Father through the Son in or with the Holy
Spirit.[58] This was naturally worked out with reference to the
spheres of incarnation, inspiration, and creation, where as we
have seen the attachment of the activity to one particular member
of the Trinity had been hesitant and vacillating from the beginning. Rufinus finds mention of all three persons of the Trinity
in the actual text of Luke 1.35 – the Holy Spirit, the Power,
and the Most High.[59] Cyril of Alexandria interprets the text
itself as referring only to the Holy Spirit, but quotes alongside it
two other texts to prove the equal participation of the first and
second members of the Trinity in the work of incarnation.[60]
The different formulae to be found in Scripture describing the
inspiration of the prophets show that it also may be ascribed to
any of the members of the Trinity; this too is evidence for unity
of substance.[61] The work of creation is the work of all three
members of the Trinity. The Father creates all things through

the Word in the Spirit, the Word being the actual agent of creation, the Spirit being the source of the power to continue in existence.[62] The Father originates, commands, or conceives, the Son creates, and the Spirit perfects.[63] The association of the Spirit with the work of creation is of particular importance, because the exclusion of the Spirit from that sphere of the divine activity was an argument being used both by Eunomius and the Macedonians against his full Godhead.[64] Didymus actually contrives to interpret a single text from the creation story as having reference to all three members of the Trinity – God the Son made man in the image of God the Father, and God the Spirit saw that it was good and blessed them.[65] Thus in these three spheres the idea of the joint activity of the persons of the Trinity, already suggested by Irenaeus, finds its full development.

Even so this does not represent the highest point in thought about the unity of the operations of the Trinity. Not merely is it heretical to exclude the Spirit from the work of creation. Any kind of division of function within the Trinity is evidence of heresy. Even the basic formula 'from the Father through the Son in the Holy Spirit' must not be regarded as an invariable descrip￢ tion of the activity of God. If it were so, it would imply the existence of a difference between the persons, which is in danger of constituting a difference of essence.[66] Thus for the Cappa￢ docians there is no difference whatever between the persons of the Trinity in their relation to the world; the only difference is to be found in their internal relations to one another. Basil describes the distinguishing characteristics as πατρότης, υἱότης, and ἁγιασμός or ἁγιαστικὴ δύναμις.[67] Gregory of Nazianzus has the most clear￢cut scheme in terms of ἀγεννησία, γέννησις, and ἐκπόρευσις, or their equivalents.[68] Gregory of Nyssa uses the terms ἀγέννητος and μονογενής for the first two persons, but then has to speak of the ἴδια γνωρίσματα of the Spirit, which he can only express negatively and periphrastically.[69] But despite these differences in terminology, they are united and emphatic about the central fact – namely that it is in this sphere of their mutual relations alone that any distinction between the persons of the Trinity is to be found.[70] As an answer to the challenge of their opponents their work represents a great achievement. In the East it was developed in terms of the doctrine of περιχώρησις; in the West it underlies the work of Augustine and his repeated insistence on the inseparability of the operations of the three persons.[71] Thus it has remained and still remains fundamental to the full orthodox doctrine of the Trinity.

None the less, it is evident that a serious difficulty remains. If there is no distinction whatever in the activity of the Trinity towards us, how can we have any knowledge of the distinctions at all? It is logically impossible, if we accept the full Cappadocian doctrine, to claim that they are known to us as a result of 'rational reflection on those particular manifestations of the divine activity which centre in the birth, ministry, crucifixion, resurrection, and ascension of Jesus Christ and the gift of the Holy Spirit to the Church'. This difficulty is not often dealt with by the fourthcentury writers themselves, because for them the same epistemological difficulty did not arise. Athanasius admits that judging solely from the facts of prophecy and of creation, one might well be led to identify the Son and the Spirit. The only reason why we must not draw that conclusion is the written form of revelation and the traditions of the faith, especially the formula of baptism.[72] In the case of the Cappadocians the problem is still more acute. Not only is there no difference in the operations, through which we might come to know of the different persons of the Trinity, but we are not even given any idea of the difference in meaning between the relationships of 'generation' and 'procession' – the only difference which is admitted to exist. It is quite clear, however, that their belief in the three persons has the same basis as that of Athanasius, with an even greater emphasis upon the baptismal formula.[73] It is therefore evident that Dr Hogdson's approach will not carry us the whole way to the fully articulated doctrine of the Trinity. The Cappadocian construction was built upon and logically requires the foundation belief that the threefold form of the Godhead is a datum of revelation given in clear propositional form.

In the light of this evidence, we seem forced to choose between three possibilities:

either (1) we do after all know about the Trinity through a revelation in the form of propositions concerning the inner mysteries of the Godhead;

or (2) there is an inherent threefoldness about every act of God's revelation, which requires us to think in trinitarian terms of the nature of God, even though we cannot speak of the different persons of the Trinity being responsible for specific facets of God's revelation;

or (3) our Trinity of revelation is an arbitrary analysis of the activity of God, which though of value in Christian thought and devotion is not of essential significance.

Of these three possibilities (1) and (2) are much more closely in accord with the general tradition of Christendom than (3), and yet both have serious difficulties. Of (1) one must simply say that it appears to conflict with the whole idea of the nature of revelation to which biblical criticism has led us. (2) is a view upheld by Karl Barth. Barth adheres strictly to the classical 'rule for theologising on the Trinity, *opera trinitatis ad extra sunt indivisa*' and affirms that 'there is no attribute, no act of God, which would not in like manner be the attribute, the act of the Father, the Son and the Spirit'.[74] He finds the root of the doc- trine of the Trinity in the statement that God reveals himself as the Lord. The meaning of this statement is to be analysed in terms of the three concepts, Revealer, Revelation, and Revealed- ness. 'The doctrine is a theoretical formulation, but one which is immediately and directly required by the statement about revelation itself.'[75] Barth says: 'If we have rejected the possibility of reading off the distinction between the three modes of exis- tence from the varieties of content in the thought of God con- tained in the concept of revelation, because in the last resort we cannot speak of such things, so now we should and must assert that the formal individual characteristics of the three modes of existence can quite well be read off from the concept of revela- tion – what actually constitutes them modes of existence –

namely, the characteristics due to their relation to one another.'[76]
This view of the source of the doctrine would not take us the
whole way to the fullest Cappadocian doctrine in that by admit-
ing a threefold distinction in the structure of every divine act it
conflicts with the Cappadocian insistence that not even the
'from whom', 'through whom', and 'in whom' of the trinitarian
formula belong exclusively to the different persons.[77] None the
less, if it could be accepted, it would certainly establish an orthodox and essential doctrine of the Trinity. But for all the advocacy
of Karl Barth, it seems impossible seriously to maintain that the
statement about revelation is something that *requires* a trinitarian
explanation. The whole argument sounds suspiciously like a
later rationalization to support a doctrine really based on (1) and
now in search of a new foundation.

(3) is admittedly revolutionary, but no more so than the
break-away from the idea of propositional revelation of which
it appears to be the logical conclusion. Even in the patristic and
medieval periods, there is a very occasional pointer to the possibility of a more than threefold analysis of the Godhead. Two
very different examples may be given. The first comes from the
ante-Nicene period when the idea of the Trinity is still closely
linked with the variety of divine activity. In one passage Hippolytus gives a number of the customary formulations – the Father
willed, the Son performed, and the Spirit manifested; the Father
commands, the Son obeys, the Holy Spirit gives understanding;
the Father is above all, the Son through all, and the Holy Spirit
in all. But together with these stands another which seems to cry
out for completion as a quaternity – the Father decrees, the Word
executes, the Son is revealed.[78] The second is from Thomas
Aquinas. Thomas is emphatic that the only distinctions within
the Trinity are distinctions of internal relation, and quite rightly
insists (as we have been insisting) that for that very reason it is
logically impossible for the doctrine to be known in any other
way than by authoritative revelation.[79] Yet the logic of his
thought forces him to postulate five notions or properties – in-
nascibility, paternity, filiation, common *spiratio*, and procession –

in God.[80] Naturally he argues that only three of these are 'personal properties'.[81] But the existence of such a discussion is sufficient evidence that even within the concept of the internal relations of the Godhead there are factors which might tend to push us beyond the number three. It is not, however, upon the validity of such admittedly tentative prefigurements that our case rests. The heart of the matter is much simpler. The 'three-ness' of the completed orthodox doctrine of the Trinity can logically be known only on the basis of a propositional revelation about the inner mysteries of the Godhead or through some other kind of specific authoritative revelation. If that basis be removed, then the necessity (though not necessarily the desirability or the value) of trinitarian thought is removed. So D. M. Edwards, starting from the premise that 'the ultimate basis on which the doctrine [sc. of the Trinity] was built is, of course, found in the New Testament, in the experience of the divine quality and potency of the historic Jesus as mediated by His living and abiding Spirit', is led on to the conclusion that 'the modern mind ... cannot see any necessity of thought for fixing on the number three, neither less nor more' and that 'no convincing reason can be given why, in view of the rich manifoldness of divine functions and activities, the number of the hypostases may not be increased indefinitely'.[82]

It might appear that the purpose of this article is entirely negative and destructive. I do not believe that that is the case. If its thesis is refuted, the refutation would necessarily involve a valuable examination of the concept of the Trinity in the light of recent epistemological ideas. If its thesis is accepted, it would represent a signal warning of the need for caution in the making of dogmatic statements about the inner life of God. In either event, there would be great positive gain.

2

Eternal Generation

The course of true doctrine never ran smooth in the early years of the Christian era. We are all familiar with the part played by ecclesiastical jealousy and imperial favour in the doctrinal history of those early centuries. Nevertheless, such factors always re-mained in one sense external to the basic story of doctrinal deve-lopment. They were enormously influential in determining what doctrines were accepted by what people at what time; they had little influence in determining the actual developing content of the thought itself. Yet even when we set on one side the vicissi-tudes of ecclesiastical or imperial influence, the course of doc-trinal development often remains somewhat rougher and more circuitous than we have been inclined to imagine. In this article I propose to illustrate this general affirmation from the curious story of the emergence of the doctrine of the eternal generation of the Son.

The traditional account of the development of this doctrine might run something like this. Generation was the natural term to use to describe the relation between the first two persons of the Trinity inasmuch as it is the obvious way of describing a rela-tionship between Father and Son. Nevertheless, in using this concept metaphorically of relations within the Godhead, certain special modifications or qualifications of its meaning were obviously required. One of the most important of such modifica-tions was the removal of the idea of temporal secondariness which would normally be associated with the Son as generated. This modification was one of the great contributions of Origen to

doctrinal development and was achieved by affirming generation to be an eternal process rather than a temporal event. In fact,
however, the development of the doctrine was very different from
this supposed picture.

In the first place the original use of the concept of generation to
describe the relation of the first two persons of the Trinity was
not very closely linked to an understanding of them as Father
and Son. This is not to say that the two sets of ideas are utterly
unrelated at the earliest stage. But in general it is true to say that
in the writings of the second-century apologists the idea of
generation is more closely linked with the ideas of God and his
Word or God and his Wisdom than with the idea of God the
Father and his Son. Thus Tatian, who never uses the concept
of Son in his *Address to the Greeks* at all, speaks there of the
Logos as becoming the first-begotten work of the Father.[1]
Similarly Theophilus speaks of God begetting his Word though
he makes very little use of the term Son.[2] It may be argued that
these writers only avoid using the term Son for apologetic
reasons, for fear that its more concrete imagery will be understood in too literal a way by those who are familiar with the
stories of the Greek gods. This is clearly implied by both
Theophilus and Athenagoras,[3] and there is undoubted truth in
the assertion; but it is not the whole truth. The original source
of the use of the term 'generation' in Christian theology lies not
so much in the fact of Christ's being known as Son, but rather
in the language already employed in the wisdom literature about
God and his Wisdom. No doubt the apprehension of God's
Wisdom as personal being through the experience of the incarnation determined the selective emphasis placed on the particular
term 'generation', but the term was already there in use in the
pre-Christian wisdom literature. Of primary importance was
Prov. 8.25, 'before all the hills he begets me'. The famous
Proverbs 8 passage is twice quoted by Justin against Trypho;
on the first occasion he quotes selectively from the whole passage
(verses 22–36); on the second occasion he carries the quotation
on just as far as the crucial words of v. 25.[4] Also significant is

Ps. 110.3, 'before the morning star I begat thee', words from a psalm which had been given an emphatic christological reference by the New Testament but which once again does not speak explicitly in terms of Father and Son.[5] Further and still clearer illustration of the way in which the ideas of generation and of Sonship could be held in relative independence of one another is to be found in the thought of Hippolytus. Hippolytus believed that the title Son could only be used properly of Christ incarnate, the preexistent Christ could only be so called proleptically and prospectively. He sums up his point by saying 'Neither was the Word, prior to incarnation and when by himself, yet perfect Son, although he was perfect Word, onlybegotten.'[6] The important point here is not the validity or otherwise of Hippolytus's particular theological view, but rather that he (the heir of the apologists) could find it natural to assert that the second person of the Godhead was before incarnation perfect Word, onlybegotten, and yet not perfect Son. For him obviously onlybegotten and Son are not logical synonyms.

So far we have been concerned only with the origin of the concept of generation in Christian theology, and the point which we have sought to make is the comparatively minor one of its relative independence of the concept of Christ as Son. This is rendered less surprising when we recall the fact, so ably demonstrated by Dr Prestige, that words derived from the root γεννάω were not rigidly distinguished from their equivalent terms derived from the root γίνομαι in the anteNicene period.[7] Obviously words of the γεννάω family could be used metaphorically without any very strong sense of their literal meaning. More striking, however, is the way in which the idea of generation once accepted came to be understood as an eternal generation.

This development is normally credited to Origen and often regarded as his greatest contribution to the development of trinitarian theology. Thus Dr Prestige writes: 'The supreme contribution of Origen to the doctrine of the Logos, that the begetting of the Son was not an event in time, but represents an eternal process within the eternal being of God, no less actual at this moment than it was before the worlds were made, seems entirely to have escaped the notice of the Arians, who drew so heavily from other aspects of his thought when he was maintain, ing the principles of extreme subordinationist theory.'[8] Similarly Dr Hodgson speaks of the 'doctrine of eternal generation by which Origen freed trinitarian theology from one element in subordinationism i.e. temporal secondariness'.[9] There is a sense in which these judgments may stand. Origen was the first to enunciate explicitly the idea of eternal generation; moreover, that idea did serve to free trinitarian theology from the idea of tem, poral secondariness with all its obviously subordinationist im, plications. Nevertheless, it needs to be affirmed far more firmly than is normally done that the idea of eternal generation played a very different role in Origen's thought from that which it was destined to play in the ultimate structure of orthodox theology. The difference might be put in this way. In Origen's scheme of thought, the primary purpose of the idea of the eternal generation of the Son was to safeguard the concept of the immutability of God the Father. In later theology its primary purpose was to safeguard the concept of the coequality of God the Son. We must attempt now to trace out the way in which this shift of function occurred.

The idea of eternal generation is very closely linked with the image of the sun and its rays; this particular implication of this particular image is firmly embedded in our minds by its presence in the Nicene creed itself with its affirmation of the Son as 'light from light'. The two are equally closely linked in the thought of Origen. In *Hom. Jer.* ix. 4, a passage surviving in the original Greek, where Origen explicitly affirms the Son's eternal genera, tion, he argues directly from the light simile. A source of light does not give birth to the light that flows from it at a particular moment only but continuously; so the Son, being the effulgence of God's glory, is not momentarily but continuously generated.[10] But while a simile may be psychologically helpful in the develop, ment of an argument, it can never be logically determinative. The issue always remains as to whether the simile continues to hold at the point newly demonstrated. The simile of the sun and its rays was originally employed by those who most certainly did not affirm the eternal generation of the Son in order to illustrate a quite distinct point – namely the possibility of derivation with out subtraction, of distinction without duality.[11] Justin indeed recognizes that the simile may not serve in every respect; he regards it as inadequate in its representation of the distinction of the persons. For this purpose, therefore, he preferred the simile of two torches to that of the sun and its rays.[12] In thus recognizing the limited potentiality of any one simile, he was entirely justified methodologically. So also no fault can be found with Eusebius's method of argument, when he argues in a precisely similar way that the sun and its rays may be a misleading simile when it suggests an eternal generation and that it needs to be corrected by the other simile of torch kindled from torch.[13] Whether or not his conclusion be correct, he would have revealed a serious weakness in Origen's case, were that case based solely upon the suggestive implications of the sun-ray simile. We must look for firmer ground as the foundation of Origen's ideas than that.

Such firmer ground is not difficult to find. At an early point in his systematic treatment of the person of Christ in the *De Principiis*, Origen poses the following dilemma. If we allow that there was ever a time when God had not generated his Wisdom, then we are bound to say that at that time God was either unable or, being able, was unwilling to generate his Wisdom. Either alternative would involve in Origen's eyes an utterly unworthy conception of God.[14] Here surely is the real ground for Origen's affirmation of the Son's eternal generation. But if Origen's argument here is valid at all, it is difficult to stop it just at that point. Certainly Origen did not do so. Later on in the *De Principiis* he uses precisely the same argument in relation to God's omnipotence. Unless, Origen argued, God at some time progressed into omnipotence (which is unthinkable), then there must always have been in existence those over whom he exercised his omnipotence.[15] Thus Origen postulates the eternal nature not only of the generated Logos, but of the whole spiritual creation.

Obviously there is a world of difference between affirming the eternal generation of the Logos as over against the creation in time of all other existents and affirming it within a system in which all rational beings are believed to be eternal existents. The idea of eternal generation as it stands in Origen's scheme of thought as a whole does not really have any effective anti/subordinationist significance at all.

This fundamental point that Origen's belief in eternal genera/tion must be seen in the context of his cosmology as a whole has been well made by Daniélou. Yet even he does not seem to allow the point its full force. He writes: 'To Origen's mind there never was a time when the Logos did not exist. On that point he could be used in anti/Arian controversy. But as he did not abandon the relation between the Logos and the *logikoi*, the consequence was that the *logikoi* too became eternal.'[16] The implication of Daniélou's words is something like this. Origen affirmed the eternal generation of the Logos for true and valid theological reasons. Unfortunately he also held a wrong belief about the nature of the relationship between the Logos and the *logikoi*. This therefore led him on to affirm a derivative belief in the eternal nature of the *logikoi* also. If this account were correct, it would follow that we have only to sever the wrongful tie between the Logos and the *logikoi*, and we are immediately left with the orthodox doctrine of the Son's eternal generation com/plete and unencumbered. But was Origen's belief in the eternity of the *logikoi* really derived in this way from a prior belief in the eternity of the Logos? It would seem truer to the evidence outlined above to say that the two beliefs were co/ordinate, independently determined by the same fundamental process of reasoning. If that be so, it is not so easy to sever the connection between them. It would seem that if one stands, both stand; if one falls, the other falls with it. Yet later theology did make just such a severance between the two beliefs. How was this done?

The doctrine of the Son's eternal generation continued to be maintained by the greatest of Origen's successors at Alexandria

in the third century, Dionysius. His assertion is based on two
main arguments – the sun and ray simile and the fact that there
had never been a time when God was not a father.[17] The first
line of argument, being argument from a simile, can have, as we
have seen, only a very restricted value. The second is in effect a
repetition of the hub of Origen's argument against the possibility of any temporal change in God. But the argument is not
without its difficulties. On the one hand it could be argued that
it did not go far enough to establish the concept of eternal
generation. The identical argument was being used at about the
same time in the West by Novatian, but to prove not eternal
generation but only the eternal being of the Son immanently in
the Father.[18] On the other hand it could be more seriously
argued that it proved too much. In the hands of Origen this
argument had indicated not only the eternity of the Son but of
the creation also.[19]

The doctrine was therefore not without its difficulties and it is
not surprising that Alexander's firm assertion of the coeternity of
Father and Son should have served to spark off the Arian controversy. The Arians are frequently accused of failing at this
point to accept and assimilate the teaching of Origen on eternal
generation, which might have saved them from their worst
errors. But perhaps after all they were closer to Origen than has
been normally recognized at this point. The basic Arian tactics
consisted in accepting the language of orthodoxy but giving it a
lower currency value. They would accept the description of
Christ as image and power of God on the ground that such
terms were also used in Scripture of men and of other created
beings; in a similar way they accepted even such terms as θεὸς
ἐκ θεοῦ, φῶς ἐκ φωτός, and even ἀληθινὸς θεός. So in particular they were prepared to accept his eternity on the ground that
Scripture implied the same of men in the words of II Cor. 4.11:
'For we which live are alway.'[20] The scriptural appeal is certainly very eccentric, but it is following in the steps of Origen
to accept the eternity of the Son but not to regard it as something
true of him uniquely.

It was not difficult to dispose of the Arian attempt to demonstrate from Scripture the eternity of other things alongside the
Son. The everlasting doors of Psalm 24, for example, are clearly
not meant to be understood as eternal in the same sense as when
the word is used of God himself.[21] But what was more urgently
needed on the anti-Arian side was a clear demonstration of the
Son's eternal nature which did not at the same time imply the
eternity of any other beings.

Methodius, who shared Origen's Platonist standpoint sufficiently to feel the force of his arguments for the eternity of creation, had argued that Origen's conclusion in this matter was not
valid because creation did not involve any change in the actual
being of God.[22] Athanasius developed this argument drawing an
explicit difference between the functions of creator and father.
The former, he argues, is an external relation and can exist
potentially; the latter is a natural relation which cannot exist
potentially.[23] In other words Athanasius appears to be claiming
that Origen's argument is valid in the case of the Son, but not
in the case of creation. But in fact when we examine the argument of Athanasius more carefully, it is evident that it really
represents a very much more radical divergence from the argument of Origen.

The starting-point of Origen's argument was God the Father
and the eternal perfection and immutability of his being. At
first sight Athanasius's argument appears to have the same fundamental form, though basing itself on the more restricted concept
of the eternity of the divine Fatherhood. Thus Athanasius
writes: 'He is ever Father and the character of Father is not
adventitious to God, lest he seem alterable; for if it is good that he
be Father but has not ever been Father, then good has not always
been in him.'[24] Or again: 'Just as the Father is always good by
nature, so he is by nature always generative.'[25] But the form of
the argument is misleading. We do not really arrive at a belief
in eternal generation through a prior knowledge of the Father's
eternal generativeness. The real starting-point for the thought of
Athanasius is not a conviction about the Father's eternal

generativeness, but a conviction about the fully and unequivo-
cally divine status of the Son. The heart of Athanasius's argument can be summarized as follows. The son is the Logos,
wisdom, and power of God in the fullest meaning of those
terms; therefore unless we are prepared to say that God was once
without reason, wisdom, or power the Son must be coeternal
with God.[26] This argument works in a different direction from
that of Origen. Origen's argument works down from the immutability of God; Athanasius's argument works up from the
divine nature of the Son.

It is true that this argument upward from the nature of the
Son does occur already in Origen. Thus in a passage of the *De
Principiis* surviving in the Greek version we read 'Let the man
who dares to say "There was a time when the Son was not"
understand that this is what he will be saying: "Once wisdom
did not exist".'[27] Nevertheless, the argument does not have the
same priority or indeed the same cogency as it does in the thought
of Athanasius. It is true, of course, that the Son was for Origen
truth, word, wisdom, light, and life. But he was these things
derivatively by participation in the Father. Indeed in so far as the
Son is truth, wisdom, and light, the Father is greater than truth,
nobler than wisdom, and superior to true light.[28] In so far as the
Father is truth, the Son is not the truth, but at most a shadow
and semblance of it on our behalf.[29] In such a setting the claim
that the nature of the Son as word, wisdom, and truth absolutely
excludes the idea of his temporal generation does not carry any
very great force. Nor in Origen's theology was it required to do
so.

Much more would need to be said if we were attempting a full
history of the development of the doctrine of eternal generation.
In particular one might go on to show how the Athanasian
argument is not only lacking in cogency when set in the context
of the earlier Origenist scheme of thought, but also difficult to
combine as it stands with later belief in a fully coequal Trinity.[30]
One would also need to discuss the significance of the terms 'will'
and 'nature' as applied to the Godhead. But my aim here has

been a much more limited one. It has been simply to demonstrate the strangely devious route by which the doctrine first
established itself in Christian theology. It is true that it was first
taught by Origen and was used as an essential weapon in the
armoury of the anti-Arians a century later. But such a statement
overlooks altogether the radical difference between its functions
in the systems of Origen and of Athanasius. It entered the stream
of Christian thought with Origen as part of a cosmology which
proved utterly unacceptable to the mind of the church. Yet only
a little farther downstream it established itself with Athanasius
as one of the most distinctive and significant of all Christian
beliefs.

3

In Defence of Arius

Abuse of one's opponent is frequently a sign of the weakness of the case that one is making out against him. It may be for this reason that, from the day when I first read H. M. Gwatkin's summary of Arianism as 'a mass of presumptuous theorizing ... a lifeless system of unspiritual pride and hard unlovingness',[1] I have felt that there may be more to be said on behalf of Arius than is usually admitted. Yet Arius remains virtually the only one of all the great heresiarchs who has received no significant measure of rehabilitation, and Gwatkin's work still stands as the authoritative work in English upon the subject. Moreover, recent articles by Dr Pollard have served only to reinforce the assessment given by Gwatkin.[2] He explicitly quotes with approval the first half of an assertion by Gwatkin to the effect that 'Arianism was utterly illogical and unspiritual',[3] and it is clear enough by implication that he would accord similar approval to the second half of the saying also.

In his article on 'The Origins of Arianism' Dr Pollard has argued for the recognition of Antiochene influence upon the thought of Arius. It is true that there are interesting points of affinity to which he is able to point and which can legitimately be used to add weight to the old tradition of his association with Lucian. But in order to establish his case, Dr Pollard claims that there are elements in the thought of Arius which are incapable of explanation in terms of a purely Alexandrian heritage. In support of this claim he points to three aspects of Arius's teaching which appear to him to be in such stark conflict with the Origenistic inheritance of the Alexandrian church as to be incomprehensible without the assumption of other influences from outside Alexandria. But in none of these cases does his argument seem to carry conviction.

The first argument is based upon the literal as opposed to allegorical tendency of Arian exegesis. 'This "selective literalism" of Arian exegesis', writes Dr Pollard, 'betrays the influence of Antioch rather than of Alexandria, where, at least until the time of Peter (*ob.* AD 310), the allegorical method continued to be favoured.'[4] But the case of Peter may well be more significant than Dr Pollard's parenthetic reference to it is intended to suggest. The general trend of Peter's theology seems clearly to have been of an anti-Origenist character.[5] A reference in Procopius's *Commentary on Genesis* suggests that this anti-Origenist character of Peter's thought may have included an element of reaction against Origen's use of the allegorical method.[6] Dr Pollard's statement certainly implies that he regards this suggestion as at least a serious possibility. But in that case it seems pertinent to recall the fact that Lucian and Peter were almost exact contemporaries, dying in the same wave of persecution within two months of one another.[7] If, therefore, the one could have been an important influence on the young Arius, so equally well could the other. Moreover, Arius was for some time closely associated with Peter. The estrangement between them which led to Peter's excommunication of Arius (if that tradition is reliable, which our evidence is insufficient to determine) was concerned not with any difference of doctrine but with the part played by Arius with regard to the Melitian schism.[8] All this is not to deny the possibility, indeed the high probability, of some Lucianic influence upon the thought of Arius. It is to deny the *necessity* of postulating some extra-Alexandrian source in order to account for the more literal nature of Arian exegesis. A further point may be made, which leads towards the same conclusion. Elsewhere Dr Pollard traces Athanasius's theological ancestry to a tradition of 'the *simpliciores* who had opposed the cosmological constructions and allegorical speculations of Clement, Origen and Dionysius'.[8] There seems therefore no logical reason why the exegetical ancestry of Arius should not be traced back to this same tradition of literalism among the *simpliciores* continuing right through at Alexandria from the time of Origen himself. Indeed it may be added that there are other aspects of Arius's thought which may have a similar ancestry. Thus Origen's explicit repudiation of the phrase 'There was when the Son was not' suggests that already in his day there were those in Alexandria who were making that affirmation.[10] Similarly Origen pours scorn on those who think of the divine Logos in too literal a way as made up of syllables.[11] Athanasius in the *Contra Gentes*, most probably to be dated before the outbreak of the Arian controversy, includes a similar attack.[12] Later still we find this view ascribed to the Arians.[13] The evidence would clearly suggest a tradition continuing among the *simpliciores* from the time of Origen and in due course picked up and used by the Arians.

Dr Pollard's second argument is expressed thus. 'Similarly the extreme emphasis on the one-ness and sole-ness of God appears to have little in common with the pluralism of Origenism'.[14] It is true that in order to bring out the difference between the Arian and the Origenistic understanding of the Godhead as a whole, it might be legitimate to speak of the greater pluralism of Origenism. But as an unqualified description of Origen's doctrine of the Godhead it is in this context seriously misleading. There is also in Origen a strong emphasis on the one-ness, and sole-ness of God. 'God is Monas, not to say Henas.'[15] 'God is wholly one and simple.'[16] While it is true that in Origen these affirmations are part of a total view of the divine nature of a graded Neo-Platonic kind, there does not seem any difficulty in envisaging a direct inheritor of such a scheme of thought developing the emphasis upon the one-ness and sole-ness of God and at the same time abandoning the idea of secondary levels of the divine nature. Indeed it would seem an antecedently probable line of development. Thus here also we do not appear to be forced to look beyond Alexandria for the parentage of Arian ideas.

Dr Pollard's third argument is the one to which he attaches most weight and which is most important for his appreciation of Arius's position. This argument turns upon 'an important distinction which the Arians made from the very beginning of their heresy, namely the distinction between the *Logos* and the *Son*. This, he goes on to argue, is in direct contradiction to the teaching of Origen, and bears only the most superficial resemblance to one aspect of Clement's teaching, so that we are forced, in Dr Pollard's judgment, to conclude that 'there is nothing in the Alexandrian tradition from which Arius' distinction could be derived'.[17] Certainly such a distinction between the Logos and the Son appears at first sight to be wholly incompatible with any theory of Origenist origins, but more careful study is needed before we can accept without question the claim that the kind of distinction which Arius draws is one that is so out of line with the drive and intention of Origen's thought that it cannot possibly be understood as a derivation from it. For this purpose a brief review of Origen's teaching about the relation of the Father and the Son will be necessary.

In his desire to maintain the absolute uniqueness and supremacy of the Father, Origen, as is well known, lays great stress on the secondary, derivative, and subordinate nature of the Son. The saying that 'the Father is greater than I' is, he declares, true in every conceivable respect.[18] And this statement is no mere declaration of a general principle; it is worked out in very specific and detailed terms. The Father alone is ὁ θεός or ἀληθινὸς θεός; the Son is simply θεός.[19] In the stricter sense of the word prayer can be offered only to the Father; prayer directed to the Son is not prayer in the fullest meaning of the word (κυριολεξία) but only in a lesser sense (κατάχρησις).[20] The gospel text that 'none is good save one, even God the Father' (to use the form in which Origen quotes the text) is evidence that the Father alone is good, whereas the Son is rather the image of God's goodness.[21] Other virtues, it is true, are applied directly to the Son; he is true light, wisdom, truth, and eternal life. This, Origen recognizes, might lead the unwary to believe there was no real difference in these respects between the Father and the Son. But this is not so; the Father is greater than the Son in all respects; he must therefore be superior to true light, better than wisdom, greater than truth, above and beyond eternal life.[22] In other words whatever can be asserted of the Son must be asserted of the Father in a transcendent degree; whatever can be asserted of the Father must be asserted of the Son only in a lesser, relative sense (καταχρηστικῶς). Origen does not apply this principle explicitly to the concept Logos. But he emphatically asserts that Logos is not to be understood as a title different in kind from all the others that are applied to Christ,[23] and he very frequently uses it in a way precisely parallel to his usage of other titles such as wisdom or truth. The logic of Origen's system, therefore, would require that if the Son is Logos, the Father must be ὑπερλογικός; and that, if the terms Logos and λογικός can be referred directly to the Father, then they can only be referred to the Son καταχρηστικῶς. If Origen himself does not explicitly draw this conclusion, is it a very difficult or unnatural conclusion for such a one as Arius to have derived in due course from the logical implications of his system? It is indeed precisely as a result of treating the concept Logos as one of the many ἐπινοίαι of the Son, parallel to wisdom, truth, etc., in an essentially Origenistic fashion that Arius is led to assert that the term is applied to the Son only καταχρηστικῶς.[24]

With Origen then there is already a clear transcendence of the Father over the Son in every respect. In the *Commentary on St John* he regards the degree of transcendence as equal to or even greater than that by which the Son and the Holy Spirit transcend all created things.[25] But in his later writings he regards the transcendence of the Father over the Son as less than that of the Son over all lesser things.[26] It is the same two clear lines of demarcation that Arius is concerned to draw. The detailed way in which he draws them is certainly different from that of Origen, but the underlying form of his thought is closely similar. I would argue, therefore, that the claim that Arianism cannot be understood in terms of a purely Alexandrian heritage has not been established.

We must ask now whether the particular form which the Origenist approach takes in the teaching of Arius deserves the measure of obloquy which has so frequently been heaped upon it. The old objection that the Jesus of Arian theory is 'neither really human nor really divine'[27] has long been shown to be an unsatisfactory form of attack upon the teaching of Arius. The argument that Arius undermined the true humanity of Jesus because he did not posit a rational human soul as part of the make-up of Jesus loses much of its force when it is recognized that in this respect his view did not differ from that of Athanasius. We shall, therefore, do better to take as a convenient form for classifying the primary objections to Arian teaching the already quoted description of it by Gwatkin as 'utterly illogical and un-spiritual'. This, moreover, accords closely with the lines of argu-ment followed more recently by Dr Pollard.

Dr Pollard's first and fundamental example of the illogicality and inconsistency of Arius's thought is 'his modification of his original statement that the Son is a creature by adding the words "but not as one of the creatures".'[28] Certainly there is something paradoxical in describing the Son as 'a creature, but not as one of the creatures', but it is not thereby necessarily to be dubbed illogical and inconsistent. The use of the word κτίζω and its derivatives to describe the origination of the being of the Son was certainly no innovation in the theological vocabulary of Alexandria. Under the influence of Prov. 8.22, one of the earliest and most favoured of testimony texts, its use had a long ancestry. It is probable that the word κτίσμα had been used in this way by both Origen and Theognostus, though in neither case is the evidence absolutely conclusive.[29] Dionysius of Alex-andria had also used similar language. The case of Dionysius is of particular interest, because his statements were explicitly chal-lenged and in defending himself he reveals the theological method and intention behind his use of such terms. In short his defence was that in dealing with more abstruse subjects one can only approach the truth indirectly with the aid of a variety of illus-trations, some aspects of which may be mutually contradictory.

Thus in this case the imagery of creation is safeguarded by its use together with the imagery of Father and Son.[30] Similarly Euse-bius of Nicomedia was to argue that creating and begetting were both metaphors to describe the indescribable, each capable of leading to error if illegitimately pressed in isolation.[31]

It is in the light of this tradition that the teaching of Arius is to be understood and the measure of its illogicality to be assessed. In his letter to Alexander Arius considers a number of words and images which had been suggested as providing a basic description of the relationship of the Father and the Son. Each he rejects because of some inherent danger that he sees within it.[32] He would indeed have been blind to true theological method if he had thought that the word κτίζω was capable of providing such a description free from all possibility of misunderstanding. But such is not the implication of his thought. Instead he pur-sues the theological method outlined in the earlier teaching of Dionysius. Whatever term is chosen is bound to be in need of qualification – even the drastic qualification of setting beside it another image which is in direct contradiction to some aspect of the original one. It is this surely which Arius intended in speak-ing of the Son as a 'creature, but not as one of the creatures'. This is not sheer illogicality, but a drastic use of the 'model and qualifier'[33] method, which is common to all theology.

If this is at all a valid account of what Arius was doing, then as well as constituting a defence of his logicality it throws im-portant light on the direction and intention of his theology. Arius's philosophical presuppositions forced him to assert a difference of οὐσία between the Father and the Son and to choose the term κτίζω as the basic description of the relationship be-tween them. But once having drawn the basic distinction in that way, his aim is to emphasize in the highest possible degree the qualifications which require to be made in the understanding of those basic distinctions. Thus, while for Arius the Son cannot *be* the Logos of God absolutely and without qualification, he is such καταχρηστικῶς and the same is true of all the other divine attributes. Similarly, while by nature he must be τρεπτός he can be and is in practice ἄτρεπτος.³⁴ In this way Arius takes the positive revelational function of the Son seriously as the εἰκών or ἀπαύγασμα of the Father.³⁵ There is no need to ascribe the positive development of the εἰκών concept as it appears in the thought of Asterius as due to a desertion of his earlier Arian position.³⁶ It is significant to notice that John 14.28 does not seem to have played a very important role in the early years of the Arian controversy. It is not one of the texts to which Athanasius found it necessary to give any thorough discussion. Origen, as we have seen, had stressed that it was true at every point of the relationship of the Father and the Son. Arius seems to have felt that the truth it represented was embodied in the single affirmation of the difference of οὐσία. Having drawn that distinction, he was as anxious as anyone to stress, within that one over-ruling difference, the similarity of character and of will between the Father and the Son. Arius certainly felt it necessary to speak of the Son as a creature, but there was no less conviction behind the qualifying words – 'but not as one of the creatures'.

The second major objection raised against the Arian system is, in Gwatkin's words, its unspiritual character. Dr Pollard makes essentially the same point by claiming that the victory of Athanasius over Arius was a victory of soteriology over cosmology.³⁷ The interpretation of Arius's thought given in the previous paragraph should give us pause before we accept this charge without question. Perhaps the clearest expression of the charge is to be found in the words of Athanasius when he writes:

By partaking of him, we partake of the Father, because the Word is the Father's own. If the Word himself were what he is by participation and were not in his own right substantial deity and image of the Father, he would not be able to deify, being himself deified. For it is impossible for one who merely possesses something by participation to pass on what he partakes to others, since what he has is not his own but the giver's, and what he receives is barely grace sufficient for his own needs.³⁸

There can be no denying that this argument has a strong appeal and that it sums up what has always been felt to be a particularly

damaging attack upon the outlook of Arius. Nevertheless it cannot be allowed to be immune from critical examination.

In the first place the argument depends upon the general principle that one can only communicate to others that which is in
the fullest sense one's own; it is not clear that this principle is
self-evidently true and it is difficult to see how it could be established. In the second place it is to be noted that the argument is
developed in terms of an understanding of salvation as deification
and that it loses something of its force if once that understanding
be abandoned. But finally even within the terms of an understanding of salvation as deification, the argument remains open
to question. The deification which is man's goal is not to become ὁ θεός but θεοὶ κατὰ χάριν. The Son, on the Arian
understanding of his person, is the prototype of θεοὶ κατὰ χάριν.
It is not clear, therefore, why he should not logically be able to
bring men to be what he is.

But even if, in the light of this line of reasoning, it could no
longer be claimed that the teaching of Arius is logically precluded from having a soteriological concern, it might yet be
argued that in fact his teaching was conspicuously lacking in this
respect. We need, however, to remember that our knowledge of
the teaching of Arius is drawn for the most part from short
doctrinal fragments chosen for polemical purposes by his opponents. We should hardly expect on such a principle of selection
to find a genuinely representative cross-section of his teaching
giving a balanced picture of any positive soteriological elements
in his thought. One needs only to compare the picture of the
christological thinkers of Antioch which we would be inclined
to deduce if we had only those extracts of their writings selected
by their opponents upon which to draw. This was indeed precisely the way in which they were interpreted by a great many
scholars in past years, but it would now be widely agreed that
their christology did enshrine a very real soteriological concern.[39]
Their soteriology was not the same as that of their Alexandrian
opponents, but it was just as real. While the evidence is insufficient for definite judgment, it is at least not unreasonable to

suggest that the same may have been true of Arius in relation to
his Alexandrian opponent.

All this is not to say that after all Arius was right, nor is it to
accuse Athanasius of illogicality or unspirituality. Counsel for
the defence does not need to smear the character of the chief witness for the prosecution. It is to suggest that the difference between
the two sides is not as absolute or as clear-cut as has traditionally
been assumed. Arius was seriously inhibited by the rigidity of
the philosophical framework within which he was operating.
As a result his teaching is certainly an inadequate account of the
fullness of Christian truth. But that is true in some degree of
every Christian theologian, ancient and modern. Even if it is
true of Arius in a comparatively high degree, it would not seem
to be in such a high degree as to merit the description 'utterly
illogical and unspiritual'.

4
The Doctrine of Christ in the Patristic Age

Patristic christology is an easy target. But easy targets breed carelessness in marksmen and many of the shafts that have been or are aimed at it in practice miss their mark. The Fathers did not desert a living response to the person of Christ and turn instead to the construction of arid formulae about him. Rather, because their response to him was so dominating a concern, they did not shirk the obvious responsibility which that faith laid upon them of loving the Lord their God with all their mind and coming to grips with the intellectual implications of their faith. In the execution of that proper and necessary intellectual task they did not regard the mysteries of the faith either as sacred preserves into which critical enquiry should not be allowed to enter or as philosophical puzzles which could be solved by the application of the rational intellect alone. It was the religious meaning of Christ for their day which was the subject-matter of their concern, and they had sufficient faith to believe that the fearless but humble application of the human mind to that task would enhance and not destroy that religious meaning and value. Nor can they justly be charged with abandoning the God-given categories of the scriptural witness and replacing them with the man-made concepts of Greek philosophy. To have refused the attempt to interpret the gospel, and therefore the person of Christ as its centre, in contemporary Hellenistic terms would have been to bind a yoke of intellectual circumcision upon the church which neither they nor we could have survived. Any deleterious influence which patristic christology may be felt to have had or still to have lies not in the task which it undertakes – *not* to have undertaken that task would have been a gross failure in Christian obedience; nor does it lie in any particular shortcomings in the way in which the task was in fact executed – I believe there were such shortcomings, and I shall try to indicate what I think some of the most important of them were, but they are of a kind that we ought to expect to find in any attempt to deal with matters of such depth and magnitude; no, the real fault is to be seen in the spirit (characteristic especially of the later periods of the patristic age) which gave to some of the early formulations of christology an absoluteness of authority to which in view of their nature they had no right to aspire or to claim.

The basic difficulty in the statement of any doctrine of Christ is that it interacts at a very profound level with so many other fundamental doctrines. Christ is a functional title. It indicates one who stands in a special relationship to God and who performs a work of ultimate significance for the life of man. It interacts therefore especially with doctrines of God and of man's condition and man's need. I stress the word 'interacts'. It is not, in my judgment, possible even to understand what sort of a thing a doctrine of Christ would be, let alone what specific form it should take, without some prior beliefs about God and the human situation. One's doctrine of Christ is bound to be formulated at the outset very largely in terms of those prior understandings. Yet it in its turn will change and modify them. There can be therefore no clear or fixed starting point. Everything is in a state of flux.

The idea of the Logos which was the key concept in the earliest expressions of christological statement in the patristic era provided a means of affirming effectively many of the things which Christians wanted to say and needed to say about Christ if they were to do justice to the experience and teaching of the church. To have lived in the Hellenistic world and not have made that link would have been to deny implicitly the universality and completeness of the church's claims about Christ. But the Logos concept was so appropriate and effective a one to use precisely because it was the focal element in an already existing complex of ideas with comparatively well-developed notions of the nature of God and of the human condition. It was these that contributed so largely to its meaning and its power. They therefore also had to be brought into a relationship of interaction with the already existing notions of Christians on those fundamental themes. The identification of Christ as the Logos was a right move provided it was seen as a first move and not as an ultimate one. The process of interaction and mutual enrichment had to go on – as indeed it did.

I have deliberately called it a process of 'mutual enrichment'. It is commonly stressed – even by those who would agree that a process of interaction with Hellenistic ideas was both inevitable and wholly proper – that the Greek conception of a metaphysically changeless God, who preserves his changelessness by means of essential detachment from the world, was one which had unfortunate consequences for Christian theology. That I would accept – provided it be also allowed that the whole process of interaction with Hellenistic thought made a contribution of substantial positive worth as well. Take one example of an important insight clarified and deepened – if not indeed newly given – by reflection on what it meant to identify Jesus with the Logos of God. Christians claimed that the touchstone of salvation for all men was to be found in faith in a man of recent times who had lived and died in an out of the way place on the periphery of the cultured world. The problem is still with us, but we do not so easily feel its emotive force – unless we stop to imagine what the faith would feel like if we were committed to proclaiming a Jesus who had lived and died in, let us say, Ceylon in the early years of the nineteenth century. Origen felt the problem in that kind of way and went so far as to admit that such words of Jesus as 'If I had not come and spoken to them, they would not be guilty of sin' would be sheer arrogant nonsense if they referred simply to the historic Jesus. Origen was very far from being prepared to admit (as the words might seem to imply) that there was no such thing as real moral responsibility or moral culpability before the time of Jesus. The words were spoken by Jesus (so Origen believed), but were only true because he was identical with that Logos or rationality which is present to all men and without which it would be meaningless to speak of guilt or blame. The claims of the gospel only carry conviction in his eyes if the one of whom the gospel speaks and who speaks in the gospel is more than a figure in history and is understood to be one who is related by his very being to the moral rationality of every man of every age.

I suggest – and clearly it is a value judgment which may well be disputed – that here we have a contribution of positive worth given to the church's understanding of Christ by the kind of process which was at the heart of patristic christological thinking. But the most central issue concerned the relationship of Christ to God. Here the concept of the Logos had a somewhat equivocal status in Greek thought. As mind or word of God the emphasis could fall either on its oneness with God, if the divine source or quality of its operations in the world needed to be stressed, or on its distinctness from God, if the eternal changelessness of God were in danger of being called into question. The identification of Logos and Son made it more difficult for the Christian to turn a blind eye on occasion to the idea of a clear distinction between God and his Logos which in certain contexts both Greek and Christian thinkers wanted to be able to do. The image of father and son naturally suggests a greater measure of distinctness than that existing between a man and his word, let alone between a man and his mind. The introduction of the personalist element in Christian thought made it much more difficult to sustain that fluidity in the concept of Logos, which had been an essential part of the role which it had played in Hellenistic thought.

Logically it might appear that two courses were open to the church. She could, with Marcellus, have played down the element of personal distinctness; she could have insisted that the Logos which was embodied and expressed in the life of Jesus was the very mind of God himself, αὐτοουσία, the divine essence itself, and restricted all talk of personal distinction, of a Father and a Son, exclusively to the period of the incarnate life. But this the church was unwilling to do. Had she not baptized from earliest times (by Christ's own command, as she believed) in the threefold name of Father, Son and Holy Spirit? Did not the high-priestly prayer of John 17 speak of an eternal sharing of glory between the Father and the Son? No, it was of the essence of the church's faith that the Logos-Son was a distinct and pre-existent being.

The obvious alternative solution was that of Arius – to accept fully the distinctness of the Logos-Son, to play down the correlative notion of eternal mind and to acknowledge that a distinct Logos-Son, though divine, can only be so in a secondary sense which is radically inferior to that of the changeless Father. But again the ordinary faith of the church would have none of it. It was the Son who was the object of popular worship, the Son who was proclaimed and believed on as the ground of salvation. Could worship be offered to or salvation received from one who was anything less than fully God? No, it was of the essence of the church's faith that the Logos-Son was divine in the fullest possible sense.

So at Nicaea the church drew the inevitable conclusion. One can hardly call it the logical conclusion, for it was in defiance of the canons of contemporary logic. The Son was an entity distinct from the Father, yet fully and equally divine with him: he was θεὸς ἀληθινὸς ἐκ θεοῦ ἀληθινοῦ. The Hellenistic conception of the Logos had enriched the church's understanding of Christ, but it had not been allowed to dominate it or to confine it to its own already existing bounds and conceptions.

Thus the theological content of the creed of Nicaea was a natural and intelligible (though not necessary, in the sense of logically inescapable) outcome of interaction between the living faith of the church and the traditional structures of Hellenistic thought. Up till that point one may properly speak of a process of development in which doctrinally speaking there are no absolutes, no definite fixed points. That is not to suggest for a moment that up till that point anything would have gone for Christian doctrine. Nothing could be further from the truth; one has only to recall the use of the rule of faith by Irenaeus or Tertullian. Yet their rule was flexible and could be expressed in a variety of different ways. But Nicaea changed all that. It wasn't *what* Nicaea said that was so new. Its content, as I have just argued, is fully explicable in the light of the preceding pattern of development. It was the *way* in which Nicaea said what it did say that was the really novel thing. Of course there had been synods and councils in the past, there had been a gradually increasing movement towards uniformity in the life of the church. But the psychological impact of the historical moment of Nicaea was enormously influential. Even in the days of perse-cution the church had regarded the imperial powers that were as ordained of God; and then, almost overnight, God's vice-regent was to be found no longer persecuting but presiding over the largest and most representative gathering of bishops in the church's history. Surely such a body in such a situation would be guided not merely to see the next step forward but to provide a firm and lasting answer on the fundamental issue of the church's faith.

I am not suggesting that that was how Nicaea impinged im-mediately on its participants. The story of synods and counter-synods, of further creeds and counter-creeds which mark the ensuing quarter-century would be unintelligible if it had done. For a variety of reasons, political and theological, Nicaea was widely resented in the years immediately after its happening. But the recrudescence of radical Arianism in the middle of the century served to reinforce and justify its affirmations. Looking back at it from the vantage point of fifty years later it stood out as a rock, different in kind and in quality from any other statement of Christian doctrine. Here was a God-given fixed point in a world of such doctrinal giddiness that a fixed standing-ground was the most obvious thing which one would be likely to ask God to give.

Now this was precisely the moment at which the christological problem in the more precise sense, the problem of the nature of the incarnate person of Christ, was coming up for more detailed discussion and debate. And for this stage of the debate it is no longer true to say that everything was in a state of flux. Now there was a fixed starting-point. The problem of Christ's person could be posed in one way and in one way only. It was the problem of how the second hypostasis of the Godhead, distinct from, yet ὁμοούσιος with the Father, the θεὸς ἀληθινὸς ἐκ θεοῦ ἀληθινοῦ, – of how he, the Logos-Son, whose eternal, fully-divine, distinct existence was already known and affirmed, had become man. However difficult the problem might prove – and it could hardly have proved more difficult than it did – there could be no going back on the terms in which it was posed.

We are so used to the incarnational problem being posed in this kind of way that we normally fail to see that there is anything particularly odd about it. It seems after all a reasonable enough procedure in a complex piece of business to settle one issue first and in the light of that decision to move on to the next issue. But it perhaps sounds less self-evidently reasonable if we alter the analogy and speak of fixing irrevocably one term in the solution of an equation before the sum has been solved or indeed been shown to be patient of any solution on that assumption. Yet that is perhaps nearer to the situation (neither analogy, of course, should be pressed) in which the christologians at the end of the fourth and beginning of the fifth centuries found themselves.

It is a recurrent theme in the christological writing of the period – and particularly in conciliar decisions of a christological nature – to claim that all that a christological account is concerned to do is to expound the faith of Nicaea. This is especially, though not exclusively, true of Alexandrian christology. Now the creed of Nicaea speaks of the eternal Son of God being made flesh, becoming man, suffering and rising on the third day. The dominant concern of Alexandrian christology was to do justice to what was there stated. The eternal Son, he who was and is ὁμοούσιος with the Father, had taken flesh and suffered for mankind. It therefore had to be affirmed at all costs that the eternal Son was the subject of all the actions and all the sufferings of the incarnate Christ. Only so could the church remain true to the faith of Nicaea and the gospel of divine salvation. This, I say, had to be affirmed at all costs. If it could not be affirmed in what might seem its most obvious Apollinarian form, it had still to be affirmed somehow or another. The cost that was paid was in fact the virtual elimination of the distinctive, individual, decision-making character of the humanity of Christ.

I do not believe that a full-blooded Alexandrian christology is a viable possibility for us today. But that makes it all the more important that we should take care not to do it any injustice. On two scores we are, I believe, always in danger of doing so.

In the first place, what seems to us an inadequate account of Christ's human nature – and indeed on our understanding of human nature may be so – need not be inadequate, at least to the same degree, on its own terms. Where that is the case, we ought to take care to stress that our complaint is not primarily with the intention of the christological construction but rather with the underlying anthropology in terms of which it was being worked out. The Platonic approach, according to which humanity as such is a more fundamental and more real concept than individual man, provided a framework of thought within which it seemed possible to make the essential Alexandrian affirmation of the subjecthood of the divine Logos throughout without destroying the humanity of Christ, or even reducing it in any really significant respect.

Secondly, it is temptingly easy to look upon the paradoxical ἀπαθῶς ἔπαθεν of Cyril as so blatantly self-contradictory that it constitutes a kind of *reductio ad absurdum*, which absolves us from the obligation of continuing to take his position at all seriously. But such a judgment again runs the risk of failing to assess his thought fairly from the standpoint of his own presuppositions. The way in which Cyril would have understood the relation between the immaterial soul of man and the experience of bodily suffering in ordinary human existence was of a kind which might well suggest that his paradox of 'impassible suffering' need not be self-evidently nonsensical. Alexandrian christology must not be too severely blamed if it fails to meet all the questions of a modern philosopher or psychologist.

Nevertheless, the conviction that there are serious difficulties inherent in the approach of Alexandria is not simply the out-come of a changed understanding of human nature in the modern era. Difficulties were also strongly felt at the time within the Antiochene school. Now the Antiochenes were facing the same questions as the Alexandrians in essentially the same terms. For them, too, the problem was the meaning of Nicaea in its affirmation of the incarnation and 'enmanment', the suffering and resurrection of the eternal and impassible Son of God. But for them the essential logic of Nicaea was the logic of the two natures. It is their continual complaint that Alexandrian talk of the Son as the subject of the incarnate sufferings must in-evitably break down the only dikes strong enough to hold back the flood waters of Arianism. A divine Son to whom suffering could be attributed could not be the fully divine Son, ὁμοούσιος with the Father, affirmed by the creed of Nicaea. For them, therefore, the thing that had to be asserted at all costs was the distinction of the two natures, a relative separation of divine and human within the one Christ.

But we have to avoid putting the Antiochene position in purely negative terms. From what has been said so far it might seem that the difference between Alexandrian and Antiochene christology was simply that, in the interaction between the gospel of divine condescension on the one hand and the conviction of divine impassibility on the other, the Alexandrians were pre-pared to allow more creative weight to the divine love. That is, I believe, a part of the story. The Alexandrians were, to their great credit, prepared to allow their religious conviction of the divine love to loosen up the stiffer joints of the existing intellec-tual framework of their ideas to a greater extent than the Antio-chenes. But it is only a part of the story. The Antiochene insistence on the genuinely human character of Christ's moral struggles and of his physical sufferings was not only motivated by jealousy for the good name of divine impassibility. It was also a religiously determined response to the meaning which they found in the story of Jesus' whole life, death and resurrection. It is a sense of affinity with that motive in their approach to christology which has led to such a growth of interest in and appreciation of their work in recent years.

But we need to beware of describing that modern approach to christology which is sometimes dubbed 'degree christology' (and of which Dr Pittenger's work is so distinguished an example) as 'Antiochene' – whether that description be intended as a compliment or as the reverse. The difference can be brought out in a way which may serve at the same time to throw light on the basic drives of both Alexandrian and Antiochene christologies in their own day, which is my primary concern in this paper. The Alexandrian starting-point was the redemptive purpose of the eternal Logos-Son, and the dominant aim of all Alexandrian christology was to reveal the form of the Logos-Son's activity in the particular, crucial stage in the outworking of that eternal purpose, which we know as the incarnation. The human life of Jesus was seen for the Alexandrian in its true light when it was seen as the temporary form of the eternal purpose of an eternal subject, the Logos-Son. From this approach flowed inevitably a playing down of the individuality of the human Jesus. In due course this worked itself out in a variety of ways – anhypostasia, enhypostasia and so forth – but it was the same dominant motif at work throughout. Now the Antiochene did not start from the exact opposite position. He shared the same devotion to Nicaea; he too insisted that the subject of the incarnation – in the sense of the act of incarnating, though not necessarily in the sense of every detailed occurrence in the incarnate life – was the Logos-Son, the second hypostasis of the Godhead. The Achilles heel of Antiochene christology was not therefore any defection from the anti-Arian position of Nicaea, any going back on the full divinity of the distinct Logos-Son; it was the

danger of parallelism, of Nestorian division, of divine Son and
human Jesus yoked together in a conjunction that seemed less
than full unity. Much modern 'degree christology', on the other
hand, seems to me to be a much more direct antithesis to the
Alexandrian approach than was the Antiochene. It tends to
take as its starting-point the empirical and historical fact of the
liberating impact of the life, death and resurrection of Jesus of
Nazareth. What it is attempting to do is to give an adequate
account of the meaning of the person of Jesus. For it, the one
thing that cannot be doubted is not Nicaea's affirmation of the
distinct existence of the eternal Logos-Son, but the fact of Jesus
as an individual, historical person. From such a starting-point
it is as difficult to affirm the role of a personal Logos-Son as
subject of the incarnate life as it was for the Alexandrian to
affirm the individual human personality of Jesus. The modern
'degree christology' ought not to be regarded as denying the
divinity of Jesus any more than the post-Apollinarian Alexandrians can fairly be described as denying his humanity; but this
will be a way of affirming the divinity, which by patristic – and
perhaps indeed by any – standards will be likely to seem as
unsatisfactory as the Alexandrian affirmation of Christ's humanity appears to most of us. But it would certainly be as fair – or,
if you prefer it, as unfair – to call him a Neo-Modalist as to call
him a Neo-Arian.

But I have strayed beyond my brief which is an essentially historical one. I have attempted to say something about the way in
which the patristic age gave expression to its conviction about
the meaning of Christ. I have attempted to do so in the most
general terms, even though the Fathers themselves pursued the
task with the utmost linguistic rigour and precision. My treatment has therefore been superficial, but sometimes surfaces are
worth looking at in order to get the picture as a whole into
perspective. The perspective I have tried to suggest to you is in
the first instance the obvious one that the Fathers' debates about
christology must be seen to have been concerned with issues of
central importance which mattered and which still matter. That

is not, of course, to suggest that we can simply carry on and treat their conclusions as our axioms – differences of world-view, of philosophical and anthropological outlook, preclude any such approach. But I have tried also to suggest a further, and I hope less hackneyed, difficulty about the whole pattern of christological work in the classical period of the fourth and fifth centuries. It seems to me that the debate between Alexandria and Antioch was being fought out with both combatants having one hand tied behind their backs. (Perhaps that was as well; they inflicted enough injury on one another single-handed, so that one shudders to think what they might have done with two.) Nicaea was a fixed point, an agreed axiom for all orthodox participants – fixed well before its implications for the further development of christology had been appreciated. And, in my judgment, it imposed a greater restriction of manoeuvring room upon the subsequent theologians than they ought to have been required to accept. It was within that particular, restricted setting that the church fought and thought its way to Chalcedon. And if my judgment is at all right on this point, it means that we cannot usefully play the fashionable game of restating Chalcedon in modern terms unless we are prepared to play with equal seriousness the less fashionable game of an equally radical restatement of Nicaea.

5

The Nature of the Early Debate about Christ's Human Soul

The New Testament writers, we are constantly being reminded, were not in the stricter sense of the word theologians. We all know what that reminder means and it is one of no small value. It would be disastrous, however, were we to allow it to suggest to us that the Christian writers of the ensuing centuries were men of an entirely different species, whose natural habitat was the study and whose primary characteristic was disinterested reflec/ tion on theological topics. Their teaching, too, can only be rightly understood in the light of the particular concerns and pressures of the moment, which impinged upon them. The importance of this approach to the study of the Fathers is par/ ticularly well exemplified by the early history of the question whether or not Christ possessed a human soul.

The question, as is well known, is one that did not come right out into the open until the time of Apollinarius. But it was not then a wholly new issue springing uncaused from the head of the great Laodicean. The question has an earlier history, but one which does not lie upon the surface of the records. It is an issue needing patient investigation if it is to be rightly understood. Earlier investigators have often been too eager to find a single, straightforward line of development. Some have found it im/ possible to believe that any of the great doctors of the church before the time of Apollinarius could have been guilty of fore/ stalling him in his heretical beliefs, and so have claimed that all orthodox writers before the time of Apollinarius did affirm the full humanity of Christ, including his possession of a rational soul. Others have argued that Apollinarius's teaching is but the natural development of the Logos theology of the second and third centuries, and that at heart the majority of earlier scholars of the Eastern Church had thought as he thought. The existence of such radically opposed views may well suggest to us that the facts are not capable of any such simple or unified explanation. If, indeed, the issue arose not so much directly, as a kind of sub-section in christological studies, but rather indirectly in a variety of contexts, then we may well expect to find a variety of answers in accordance with the different contexts within which the question arose.

The apologists and other early or mid-second-century writers do not provide very fertile ground for our investigations. There is no doubt that the orthodox writers of the period intended to affirm that in the incarnation Christ became fully man. But no deductions can be drawn simply from the general nature of the language in which that affirmation is framed. The use of the word 'flesh' to describe Christ's human nature is wholly incon-clusive; it was regularly used by Tertullian who, as we shall see shortly, undoubtedly affirmed the fact of Christ's possession of a human soul. Conversely, where writers speak of Christ becom-ing man, rather than using the term flesh, it cannot simply be assumed that this involved either the conscious conviction that he possessed a human soul, or even that such writers would cer-tainly have affirmed the fact had the issue been clearly and pre-cisely formulated and put to them. One famous passage in Justin Martyr, where he speaks of Christ becoming 'the whole rational being, both body and logos and soul', obviously bears upon the matter, but it has proved notoriously difficult to inter-pret.[1] Dr Raven understood this to mean that 'the Logos in Him took the place of the highest element, the λογικόν, in us'.[2] E. R. Goodenough, however, claims with equal confidence that it shows Justin to have believed that 'in the incarnation the Logos became a man in all three respects, body, soul and Logos or spirit'.[3] It is doubtful whether Justin himself had any clear or precise opinion on the subject. Certainly the writings of his which have come down to us do not enable us to form any definite judgment on the matter. It is with the anti-Gnostic writers at the close of the century, with Irenaeus and Tertullian, that the issue begins to emerge into the open and our investigation proper is able to begin.

The Gnostics, against whom Irenaeus and Tertullian wrote, most certainly did deny the full humanity of Christ. In opposing them, the orthodox writers were not simply concerned with securing a satisfactory description of Christ's person. They were far more concerned to insist that Christ's humanity must have been complete for man in his totality to be saved. The principle lying behind their concern about the wholeness of Christ's human nature is the famous Irenaean principle, expressed in the preface to Book v of his work against the heresies, that 'he became what we are in order that he might bring us to be even what he is himself'. Irenaeus goes on to develop this principle in the succeeding chapter to include the notion that he gave his soul for our souls, his flesh for our flesh.[4]

As these ideas were being developed with a consciously anti-heretical purpose, the emphasis in the teaching of Irenaeus and Tertullian is determined by the nature of the denials of the heretics against whom they were writing .These were concerned with the flesh rather than with the soul. Thus, the point that is made continually by Tertullian is that Christ's taking of our flesh is the necessary means of that flesh's purification and ultimate redemption.[5] He does not need to stress Christ's taking of a human soul to the same extent, for the obvious reason that it was not a bone of contention between him and the great majority of Gnostic writers. 'The salvation of the soul', he writes, 'I believe needs no discussion; for almost all heretics, in whatever way they accept it, at least do not deny it. We may leave to his own devices the one solitary Lucan, who spares not even this entity'.[6] Thus the question did not seem to Tertullian to require detailed discussion. But it is clear enough that his attitude to Christ's possession of a human soul is essentially the same as in the case of his physical body. The soul receives only occasional specific mention, but the affirmations on those occasions are clear and definite. They arise at times in discussion with heretics who, even if not denying Christ's soul altogether, understand it in such a curious sense as to merit the attack of Tertullian's pen.[7] At other times they arise as a natural corollary in discussions concerned primarily with the flesh. Thus, with curious exegesis, Tertullian insists that Christ will lose nothing of that which the Father has given him, but will raise up at the last day the whole humanity which he received – both body and soul.[8] Moreover, Tertullian found his belief clearly expressed in the plainest words in the gospel record. There is no forcing of exegesis in his quoting Matt. 26.38 and John 6.51 as evidence of Christ's possession of both soul and flesh.[9]

The position of Tertullian on this score, then, is clear enough, even though it is not laboured as heavily as some other aspects of his theological convictions. The basic motive of his thought upon the matter is soteriological. The famous anti-Apollinarian principle of Gregory Nazianzen that 'what is not assumed is not healed' is already there in the writings of Tertullian. As with so much else in the field of christological thought, the West never shifted far from the position mapped out by Tertullian at this early stage in the development of doctrine. We have comparatively little Latin literature of a strongly theological character between the time of Tertullian and the period after Apollinarius, when the matter of Christ's possession of a human soul was no longer a genuinely open question. Hippolytus expresses the same belief as Tertullian for the same fundamental soteriological reason.[10] Both Victorinus and Hilary explicitly affirm the fact and make use of it in anti-Arian argument in a way similar to that used by the Antiochene writers in the East.[11] It has been claimed that Novatian implicitly denies the fact when he argues that 'if the immortal soul cannot be killed or slain in any other, although the body and flesh can be slain, how much rather assuredly could not the Word of God and God in Christ be put to death at all although the flesh alone and the body was slain'.[12] Dr Kelly regards the evidence as 'decisive'.[13] But the claim of d'Alès that Novatian is here using an *a fortiori* argument, which does not necessitate his having believed that the divine Word in Christ took the place of the soul in other men, would appear to provide a perfectly possible alternative explanation.[14] In view of the unqualified unanimity of Latin writers on the issue, apart from this one possible case, d'Alès's explanation has much to commend it.[15] If indeed d'Alès is right, then the development of the doctrine in the West provides a very simple and straight-forward story. When we turn to the Eastern Church, however, the development proves to be a very much more complex business.

We may start our investigation of Eastern thought with the person of Origen. The first point to be noted is that we find in Origen the same basic affirmation and the same basic reasoning about Christ's human soul that we find in Tertullian. In the *Dialogue with Herakleides*, Origen (using a trichotomist anthropology) argues explicitly on soteriological grounds for Christ's having assumed each part of our human nature. He sums up his argument with the words: 'The whole man would not have been saved unless he had taken upon him the whole man'.[16] Moreover, as with Tertullian, this soteriological reasoning is supported by the direct testimony of Scripture. For this purpose the basic trio of gospel texts (John 10.18; 12.27 and Matt. 26.38) is supplemented by the addition of words from the christologically interpreted Psalm 22.21.[17] In the *Commentary on John* soteriological reasoning and gospel evidence are combined so as to bring out the importance of the experiences ascribed in the gospel records to Christ's soul for the healing of the souls of men.[18] In the case of Tertullian and other Western writers this represents virtually the sole and complete significance of the question of Christ's human soul. But with Origen this is very far from being the case. The idea plays an important role in two other related realms of theological thought, which are more closely concerned with the manner of the incarnation.

The first of these can be dealt with comparatively briefly. In the light of his belief in the pre-existence of souls, Origen taught that Christ's soul alone remained free from sin, continuing in perfect association with the divine Logos.[19] In this kind of way Origen was enabled to fit his idea of the full incarnation of Christ into his whole perspective of the eternal existence and pre-cosmic fall of human souls. But this insistence on the eternal perfection of Christ's human soul did lead Origen to speak on occasion as if the self-emptying condescension of Christ, which lies so close to the heart of the gospel, was to be understood not simply of the divine Word but also of Christ's human soul. Thus, on occasion, he appears to apply the words of Phil. 2.6–7 to Christ's human soul, though this is not his normal interpretation, nor is it intended to be exclusive of the application of the passage also to the divine Word.[20] To later generations, and especially to Jerome, this interpretation of Phil. 2.6–7 was a matter of grave offence.[21] Nevertheless, the issue is not of great importance for the development of ideas concerning the basic question whether or not Christ possessed a human soul. Those who reacted against this aspect of Origen's teaching on the subject did not on that account need to deny that Christ possessed a human soul. They needed only to deny the pre-existence of souls, which they were anxious enough to do on many other grounds also.

The second way in which the idea of Christ's human soul entered into the thought of Origen was very much more significant for the immediately subsequent development of the doctrine. Origen saw the soul of Christ as playing a vital mediating role in the effecting of the incarnation. It appeared to him to avoid the crudity, not to say the impossibility, of the idea of a direct union between God and flesh. The idea of a union between the Logos and a human soul, and also the idea of the presence of a soul within a human body were both fully intelligible and acceptable ideas.[22] Thus, Christ's human soul was significant for Origen, not merely as providing assurance about the salvation of our human souls, but also as serving to make the concept of Christ's incarnate person more readily intelligible. The use of the idea by Origen in this context was immensely significant in determining the attitude of ensuing generations to the whole concept.

Two incidents in the years between the death of Origen and the eruption of the Arian controversy indicate the trend of thought on this topic during that period. The first of these is the attack by Malchion and those associated with him on the teaching of Paul of Samosata. If the opponents of Paul can justly be described as Origenists acting in accordance with Origenist principles in their objection to the monarchianism of Paul, they were certainly not following Origen in their objection to the christological aspect of his teaching. They were vehemently opposed to Paul's radical separation of the Logos and the man Jesus, which resulted in a conception of the union brought about by the incarnation as something less than a union κατ᾽ οὐσίαν.[23] They insisted in reply that just as men are made up of flesh and something in the flesh, so Christ is made up of the divine Logos in a body like ours.[24] More emphatically still they asserted that the one, admittedly very important, difference between Christ and us is that the divine Logos takes the place with him which the inner man holds in our make up.[25] This last saying certainly seems to imply that the divine Logos replaces the rational human soul in the case of the person of Christ. Thus, whereas to Origen the assertion of Christ's possession of a human soul within the context of the understanding of the unity of his person seemed a positively helpful, even necessary, idea, to the majority of those who followed him, particularly, indeed, to those who in other respects were largely continuators of his thought, the idea seemed a liability or worse.

A second instance helps to substantiate this interpretation of the development of ideas in the years after Origen. Early in the fourth century Pamphilus composed a work in defence of Origen. He divides up the various charges made against him under a series of headings. One of these is entitled, 'Quod unus est Christus filius dei'. It is in the course of this section that he mentions the objection that Origen speaks of Christ's human soul. Whereas, on most issues, he is the wholehearted champion of Origen against his critics, he seems to regard this objection as one of the more reasonable complaints being raised against the memory of Origen. He does not deny the charge nor does he argue directly for the truth of Origen's belief. Instead, he simply declares that Scripture talks in the same way of Christ's soul, and that Origen is hardly to be blamed for using language which is after all the language of Scripture.[26]

Other writings of the same period are less conclusive in their testimony, but, on the whole, they lend support to the idea that the development which we have been tracing was very widely and generally held.[27] Certainly there is sufficient evidence to conclude that the notion of Christ's human soul was found to be an embarrassment within the context of the attempt to conceive the unity of Christ's person. Nevertheless, Scripture did speak in such terms and, therefore, the idea was allowed to drop tacitly out of use rather than be directly and explicitly denied.

The importance of the text of Scripture as keeping alive the possibility of thinking in terms of Christ's human soul is well illustrated by Pamphilus's collaborator in the defence of Origen, Eusebius of Caesarea. He not only makes no use of the idea of Christ's human soul in his own theological writing, but he comes very much nearer than other writers of the same period to outright denial of it.[28] But, in spite of this, there are occasions when he does use the term; those occasions, as de Riedmatten has pointed out, are always closely related to comment on the biblical text.[29] It is amusing to reflect that, had Origen himself not believed for other reasons in the existence of Christ's human soul, the mere word of Scripture would have been for him a testimony easily overcome. Indeed, Origen points to the fact that Scripture speaks of the soul of God, which must be allegorically understood, and also that some exegetes have interpreted Christ's reference to his soul in the gospel record as an allegorical reference to the apostles, in view of the fact that they represent the best part of his body, the church.[30] Origen would have had no

difficulty in accepting such exegesis had his doctrinal convictions predisposed him to wish to do so. Epiphanius, indeed,
asserts that the first of these two lines of defence – to wit, the
argument that the phrase should be understood allegorically on
the analogy of the soul of God – was used by the Arians.[31] It is
perhaps more likely that the argument should be attributed to the
Apollinarians.[32] In any event, it is to the credit of the main body
of Christian thought in the late third and early fourth centuries
that such reasoning, even though it might have suited their case,
was considered too far-fetched to have any appeal.

Such, then, was the climate of thought within which the
Arian controversy arose. This background of ideas is an essential
preliminary to a true understanding both of the appeal of Arian
ideas and also of the way in which that teaching was opposed,
especially by Athanasius. When Arius argued that in the light
of his ignorance of the day of the Parousia, his dereliction upon
the cross and his life of prayer the Son must be a creature and
not eternally co-existent with the Father,[33] he did not have first
to demolish the belief that Christ possessed a human soul before
his syllogisms would be felt to carry weight. The majority of his
first opponents, as well as of his first supporters, held no such
belief. For the same reason no surprise ought to be felt when it is
shown that Athanasius did not make use of the concept of
Christ's human soul as a way of countering the teaching of
Arius.[34] The approach of Athanasius needs to be understood
in the light of the immediately preceding teaching of the late
third century, not in the light of the subsequent teaching of
Apollinarius.

With Eustathius the position was different. Though he would
have relished the description no more than would any other
orthodox fourth-century thinker, he stood much closer to the
tradition of Paul of Samosata. For him it was quite clear that the
kind of thing which Arius attributed to the divine Word could
not possibly be attributable to so fully divine a being. It must
be ascribed to Christ's human nature as something other than
the divine Word. Moreover, in view of the mental, emotional

and volitional experiences involved, that human nature must have included the existence of a rational human soul.[35] In so insisting Eustathius was going against the stream of much contemporary thinking, but he was thereby enabled to give a much clearer and more convincing answer to Arian reasoning than Athanasius was in a position to do. Moreover, he stood in the ancient tradition of Tertullian and Origen. Tertullian had ascribed all such mental human experiences to Christ's flesh. It is the flesh, he says, which was 'sorrowful even unto death', with an obvious reference to Matt. 26.28 where the gospel text has the word 'soul'.[36] For Tertullian, as we have seen, the word flesh implies the whole of Christ's human nature. If he does not bother, in this context, to make explicit mention of Christ's human soul, it is simply that there was no need to assert what no one was then wishing to deny. Origen also used the same line of answer to the problem of the more lowly state of the incarnate Christ, and on occasion he does make explicit reference to Christ's human soul in this context.[37]

In the light of this whole line of development the great crux of interpretation for this subject, the decision of the synod of Alexandria under the chairmanship of Athanasius in 362, becomes somewhat easier to understand. The crucial passage is to be found in the *Tomus ad Antiochenos*, vii. In it Athanasius is consciously mediating between two groups, which were both anti-Arian but which were in disagreement on other points, including the christological issue with which we are concerned. The passage reads:

Since certain seemed to be contending together concerning the fleshly economy of the Saviour, we enquired of both parties. And what the one confessed, the other also agreed to – namely, that the Word did not, as it came to the prophets, so dwell in a holy man at the consummation of the ages, but that the Word himself was made flesh, and being in the form of God took the form of a servant, and from Mary after the flesh became man for us, and that thus in him the whole human race is perfectly and wholly delivered from sin and quickened from the dead and given access to the kingdom of heaven. For they confessed also that the Saviour had not a body without a soul (οὐ σῶμα ἄψυχον), nor without sense or intelligence; for it was not possible, when the Lord had become man for us, that his body should be without intelligence, nor was the salvation effected in the Word himself a salvation of body only but of soul also.

Athanasius is here mediating between the successors of Eustathius, who strongly affirmed the existence of Christ's human soul, and those who stood more directly in the tradition of Malchion and the main body of Eastern thought in the early fourth century including Athanasius himself. What stands out clearly from the passage is that the difference of conviction be-tween the groups is closely related to the different contexts within which they posed the problem. Those who were unhappy about the ascription of a human soul to Christ were unhappy about it, as we have seen all along, when they related it to the question of the unity of Christ's person. Set within that context it seemed to destroy the uniqueness of the incarnation and set it on a level with the inspiration of the saints. This was a difficulty felt deeply by Athanasius himself, and he, as much as anybody else, would have needed the reassurance given in the first half of the passage quoted.[38] The Paulinians, on the other hand, based their case on the soteriological importance of Christ's human soul.[39] 'The salvation effected in the Word himself was not a salvation of body only but of soul also'. In so doing they were appealing to the fundamental line of reasoning which, as we have seen, deter-mined the first explicit insistence upon the idea in the writings of Tertullian and Origen. This whole line of thought seems to have been largely overlooked during the period when serious mis-giving was being felt over the implications of the concept of Christ's soul for an understanding of the unity of his person. It had not, of course, been entirely forgotten. Those who, like Eustathius, had found the concept of Christ's human soul necessary for the refutation of Arianism had not wholly ignored its particular soteriological emphasis, but the idea had not been greatly stressed.[40] Its emphatic reintroduction at this point into the main stream of debate was of vital importance. It is this which seems to have weighed with Athanasius, enabling him to find reconciliation with the Paulinians with a good conscience. It is doubtful, even so, whether he went all the way with their argument. The crucial words οὐ σῶμα ἄψυχον need not have signified for him the existence of a specific human soul distinct from the divine Logos. But, at least, the soteriological line of argument was successful in persuading Athanasius that the Paulinians were brothers to be embraced in Christian fellowship. He himself never seems to have taken the idea of Christ's human soul over into his own theological thinking. It is true and significant that we do find him in a later writing repeating the soteriological argument that Christ's incarnation was a full and real incarnation, and that it needed to be such for him to save the whole man, soul and body. But even in that context he does not find it necessary himself to assert Christ's assumption of a specific human soul as an explicit element in that full incarnation.[41]

Thus, the significance of the *Tomus ad Antiochenos* is that it reveals the resurrection of the original soteriological argument as the one way in which the main body of the Eastern Church was enabled to feel at all at home with the idea of Christ's human soul. From that point on the argument dominates the scene and sweeps all before it, including above all Apollinarius.

Apollinarius is quite explicit in his disavowal of the idea of Christ's human soul. To accept the idea is, for him, to be following in the footsteps of the hated Paul of Samosata.[42] Indeed, he goes further than his predecessors in claiming that the notion is not merely one which renders thought about the unity of Christ's person inadequate, but one which renders it altogether inconceivable. The idea is not merely false: it is a logical absurdity.[43] With convictions of such strength on the question of the unity of Christ's person, no *rapprochement* was possible with those who held to the belief in Christ's possession of a human soul so strongly on soteriological grounds. Apollinarius, indeed, is not content simply to challenge the idea of Christ's human soul on grounds of its impossibility from the point of view of the unity of Christ's person and to pass over the question of its claimed soteriological role in silence. He goes far beyond any of his pre-decessors in attacking the idea on directly soteriological grounds as well. Every human soul, in his view, is by nature τρεπτός – fallible, unstable, a prisoner of corrupt imaginations, constantly succumbing to the flesh which it ought to be controlling. If Christ, therefore, had a human soul or mind, he would have become enmeshed in this morass of τρεπτότης; he could not have been a Saviour from it. What man needed for salvation was the replacement of his τρεπτός-soul or mind with one that was by nature ἄτρεπτος. This was what happened in the person of Christ. His possession of a human soul would necessarily have precluded him from being an effective Saviour of fallen man.[44]

But this attempt to do away with the idea of Christ's human soul even in the realm of direct soteriological concern had no chance of success. The various Apollinarian arguments were met with appropriate counter arguments. But clear and loud above all other lines of reasoning stood out the age-old conviction that 'that which he has not assumed, he has not healed'.[45] As another writer puts it more fully, 'he gave his body for men's bodies, his soul for men's souls'.[46] In much earlier stages of development, Christ's human soul had been firmly acclaimed on these same soteriological grounds. Doubt had been thrown on the idea because of the difficulty of fitting it into the distinct context of concern for an adequate conception of the unity of Christ's person. When the two contexts could no longer be kept apart, there was no question which weighed more heavily with the main body of the church. Nothing could shake the solid convic-tion of the fundamental soteriological argument for the existence of Christ's human soul.

From this time on, therefore, the basic issue was finally and irrevocably settled. It was no longer possible to deny the fact of Christ's possession of a human soul and hope to remain within the fold of the orthodox Christian fellowship. But there was still room for considerable variety in the way in which that basic fact could be affirmed and used in the thought of different writers. In the final section of this article, therefore, we shall aim to show how varied was the way in which the idea of Christ's human soul was used by different writers in the immediate post-Apollinarian era, even though they were in full agreement about the basic fact.

We may start with the christology of the *Commentary on the Psalms* discovered at Tura, which has been the subject of an exhaustive study by A. Gesché and which may be ascribed with a very high degree of probability to Didymus the blind. The author affirms the existence of Christ's human soul with a considerable degree of precision and confidence. Its soteriological significance is not central to his purpose, but it is clearly recognized.[47] Yet, as Gesché repeatedly points out, the one striking gap in his theological construction is the way in which he virtually ignores altogether the question of the manner of the co-existence of the two natures in the one person of Christ.[48] There are hints that he might have liked to follow the line of Origen's thought upon this matter, as in other respects he does much more closely than most scholars of his age – even to the point of accepting the idea of the pre-existence of souls.[49] But, by and large, the whole question is left entirely on one side. The idea of Christ's human soul did not fit happily into the context of the unity of Christ's person.

The nature of the unity of Christ's person, however, was not the kind of issue that could simply be passed over in silence in that way. The main thinkers of the Antiochene and Alexandrian schools were very alive to the problem. Both schools clearly affirmed Christ's possession of a human soul; both gave to it a soteriological significance. But they did so in markedly different ways. In the case of the Antiochenes the role of the human soul was an active one: in the case of the Alexandrians it was almost wholly passive.[50] While for the former the temptations and emotional struggles recorded of Jesus show his human soul emerging unscathed and victoriously triumphant, for the latter they show the divine Logos effecting a divine conquest in the sphere of our human weakness. If we ask why such writers as

Cyril, having once accepted the fact of Christ's human soul, did not go on to make more positive use of it – for example in anti-Arian debate – the answer is clear enough. Cyril stood firmly in the tradition of Athanasius in two senses. In the first place, Athanasius had provided a way of interpreting the life of Christ which made no explicit reference to Christ's soul but which still dealt with Arian objections and had a vigorous soteriological content. If to our ears his interpretation seems harsh and unsatisfactory, for Cyril it was the basic substance of his theological upbringing and something from which he was not likely to move very fast or very far. And, secondly, the other context of the unity of Christ's person could not be wholly forgotten or ignored. If Christ's soul had to be affirmed for soteriological reasons, let it at least be affirmed in a way as little inimical to the unity of Christ's person as possible. This could best be done if its soteriological role was conceived in purely passive terms, not as an active agent but as the sphere in which a divinely wrought salvation was effected and received. Thereby not only was the divine nature of the salvation clearly empha-sized, but the idea of Christ's human soul could virtually be ignored in the consideration of the unity of Christ's person.

Thus, we can see in Cyril a fitting culmination of the course of development we have surveyed. Our contention is that, from the very start, the mind of the Fathers was clear that when think-ing soteriologically they must affirm the fact of Christ's possession of a human soul. On the other hand, when thinking of the unity of Christ's person they were (with, as so often, the vigorous exception of the boldly individual mind of Origen) almost equally clear that the idea must be repudiated. Earlier writers tended to emphasize one context to the virtual exclusion of the other, according to the concerns of the moment which confronted them. The case of Apollinarius revealed once for all that if the two contexts are brought face to face with one another, then it is the soteriological context, with its affirmation of Christ's human soul, that will predominate. In Cyril of Alexandria one can see an attempt to combine the two insights. Few, I think, can feel that the resultant picture as worked out by Cyril is wholly satisfactory. Is this then an irreducible and inescapable contra-diction in the thought of the Fathers? If we believe that the human soul is a clear and specific entity, the difference between whose existence and non-existence can be precisely understood and defined, then we will have to say that it was a very serious flaw in the whole structure of early Christian thought. If, on the other hand, we believe that the soul cannot be understood in such objective, substantival terms, but rather that it is a necessary (but sometimes misleading) element in talking about the mysteries of human existence, then who is to say that the Fathers were wrong in their clear conviction that in some contexts it needed to be affirmed of Christ, but in others to be denied?

6

The Theological Legacy of St Cyprian

'Into theology Cyprian scarcely ever entered', wrote W. D. Niven,[1] yet d'Alès's book *La Théologie de S. Cyprien* covers more than four hundred pages without appearing to be dealing with a non-existent subject.[2] The *prima facie* conflict is not difficult to resolve. A religious leader can no more help talking theology, whether consciously intending to do so or not, than Molière's M. Jourdain could help talking prose. An unconscious theology, indeed, can be every bit as important and as influential as a fully self-conscious one; in fact, its influence is very liable to be the greater, because succeeding generations are less likely to be aware of it and so less likely to submit it to critical scrutiny and review. In no case is this largely unconscious influence more significant than in the case of Cyprian. All the other outstanding writers of the third-century Western Church ended their days in schism. Tertullian, Hippolytus and Novatian were all far greater theologians than Cyprian, but all three broke from the catholic church in support of the rigorist cause. In spite of this fact, their importance for later theology remains considerable. But that importance is a fully conscious theological one. Where their ideas were accepted and developed, it was because they carried conscious conviction as theological ideas; the fact of who it was who was the father of the ideas did little to commend them. But with Cyprian the case is altogether different. Not only does he stand out as the only substantial

Western writer of the third century to avoid the sin of schism, but his words had the added prestige of being the words of an outstanding bishop and, still more importantly, martyr. It is not without significance that he is the first Christian to be the subject of a biographical study and that he should be the only non-Roman to receive specific mention by name in the Canon of the Roman Mass. Thus the influence of Cyprian's teaching was immensely enhanced by the prestige of his person. Moreover, that teaching belonged to so early a period in the life of the church that its influence was able to affect not only the conscious theological formulations of other scholars, but the unconscious presuppositions of Western Christian thought. The nature of his influence is, therefore, a subject that would seem to demand particularly careful study. We cannot allow our respect for Cyprian's person to determine our judgment as to the soundness of his theological influence. O. D. Watkins, in his work on the history of penance, argues that 'Cyprian was a faithful servant of God; and it may be expected that God acted through him in the determination of courses of action which gave direction to the Church of all time'.[3] But just as it is clear (*pace* Cyprian) that the efficacy of a sacrament is not to be determined by the worthiness or unworthiness of the minister, so also it is clear (*pace* Watkins) that the validity of a theology is not to be determined by the worthiness or otherwise of the theologian. Cyril of Alexandria was far too good a theologian for any such theory to be tenable.

None the less, even though the worthiness of the theologian be no guarantee of the value of his theology, a knowledge of his personal history may still be an important factor for the understanding of his theology. Our knowledge of Cyprian's life diminishes steadily as one tries to work one's way back from the moment of his death. We have very full records of his martyrdom, a comparatively full account of his episcopate, a lesser knowledge of his life as a Christian before becoming a bishop, and very little knowledge indeed of his pre-Christian days. His biographer, Pontius, regarded the moment of his second birth as the most suitable point at which to begin the record of his life and death.[4] Of his first birth, therefore, we have no certain knowledge. The date customarily given is between about AD 200 and AD 210, but this is no more than a guess based on the fact that he would seem to be a man well-established in his career and in society at the time of his conversion. Of this fact there can be little doubt; and it is this fact, rather than any guess as to the actual date of his birth, that is important – indeed, I would suggest, more important for an understanding of his theology than has usually been recognized. He was evidently a man of wealth with a considerable personal fortune. He seems to have had a good general education and, in particular, a thorough training in rhetoric. The profession of an orator he followed with no little success and honour. Morever he would seem to have enjoyed the friendship of some of the leading citizens of Carthage – a friendship which continued in some measure right up to the time of his death. Our evidence in building up this picture is often indirect and uncertain in detail, but the general outlines are clear enough – a man of well-established standing and repute in the affairs of the city of Carthage.

Such was the man who was converted to Christianity about the year AD 246. We cannot be sure of the precise date, but he could still be described as a neophyte at the time of his elevation to the episcopate in 248. Of that conversion we have his own account in the work entitled *Ad Donatum*. It is written in a highly rhetorical style, and due allowance has to be made for this fact in its interpretation. Cyprian speaks of 'the innumerable errors of my previous life', of being 'disposed to acquiesce in my cling-ing vices' and of 'indulging my sins as if they were actually parts of me'.[5] Nevertheless, one does not sense the personal anguish of soul which so clearly shines through the also highly rhetorical account of the conversion of that later North African bishop, Augustine. The total impression is of a man who has always lived an upright and serious life, turning in despair from the corruptions and licentiousness of pagan society and looking to the church as the place where his ideals show more signs of real acceptance and effective implementation. The influence of Seneca to be traced in some of his writings is probably indicative of the source of the ideals which had motivated him even in his pre-Christian days. All in all the cry of 'woe' embodied in the *Ad Donatum* would appear to spring more from his sense of dwelling among a people of unclean lips than from an intense personal sense of the uncleanness of his own lips.

Thus, the record of Cyprian's conversion does not suggest to us the presence of a deep transformation of personal life or moral ideals. But this is not to deny the very radical nature of the transition from membership of pagan society to that of the Christian church. Immediately after his baptism Cyprian gave away in alms a considerable proportion of his worldly possessions. This was in a sense symbolic of the absolute break with his old life which he clearly intended to make. It is a striking fact that, unlike so many other North African writers, he avoids altogether quotations from pagan writers. It is as if he wished to give away not only the material inheritance of his pagan days but to give away its literary inheritance also. But if that were his intention, it was a task not so easily achieved. He may have succeeded in eschewing pagan literary quotations; he certainly did not abandon the rhetorical style of his pre-Christian days, and it is at least open to serious question how far he abandoned the underlying presuppositions of his earlier thinking.

What then did he seek to put in place of the pagan literary tradition upon which he was trying to turn his back? The answer would seem to be, in short, the Bible and Tertullian. Philosophy seems to have had little attraction for him. His approach to the Bible, as exemplified both by the form of the three books of *Testimonies* and by his writings at large, is that of the plain man who collects a series of texts to provide clear-cut answers to the theological, and still more the practical, questions of the moment. Of earlier Christian literature, there is little evidence of his knowledge of anything outside the writings of Tertullian, the 'master' whose works he is traditionally reported to have studied daily and whose influence upon him was enormous. In Tertullian he would have found, admittedly among many other things, a kindred mistrust of philosophical argument and a similar insis' tence upon the literal, even legalistic, meaning of the biblical text.

It is not easy for a man in middle age to change the whole tenor of his thinking. Cyprian's intention to make a clean break with his pagan past is evident enough. What is not so evident is that he had either the capacity or the opportunity to make that break effective at the deeper levels of his thinking. A man of good education, but no strong philosophical bent, finds in middle age that the Christian church provides the practical answer to the moral and social ideals which his own society has raised in him but has failed to satisfy. He comes over into a Christian tradition which is based on a non'philosophical use of the biblical text as providing a clear'cut and distinctive framework of belief and practice. It is not surprising that such a man in the short period of twelve years, largely taken up with intensely pressing and difficult practical decisions, should not have developed into a profound Christian theologian. His election to succeed Donatus as bishop of Carthage in 248 may, in spite of the warning of the pastoral epistles about selecting neophytes for episcopal office, have been a wise one for the immediate purpose of steering the church of Carthage through the troubled seas of the Decian and Valerianic persecutions. But history has cast him for a wider role, that of influencing at a very deep level the theological thinking of the Western Church for the subsequent seventeen hundred years. It is by no means so clear that his very evident qualities were such as to equip him for this larger task. It is in the light of this understanding of his personal character and experience that we must review his theological teaching and influence on the later thinking of the church.

By far the most famous aspect of Cyprian's thought is his ecclesiology; of all his sayings the most often quoted must be 'Extra ecclesiam non salus est' and 'He that hath not the church for his mother cannot have God for his Father'. He is tradition' ally known as the classic exponent of the doctrine of the visible church as the one and necessary ark of divine salvation. All this is true, and if our concern was to give a balanced and systematic account of Cyprian's thought as a whole, these ideas would need to be developed at some length as the hub and centre of all his thinking. But this has been done many times over and does not need to be done yet again here. Moreover, in this respect Cyprian is neither markedly original nor in the long run so very influential. Cyprian's basic view of the church is one that was common to virtually all Christian thinkers of the early centuries. Cyprian, as a result both of his own background which prompted him to see the church as a clear-cut sociological entity over against pagan society and also of the circumstances of state persecution with which he had to deal, no doubt drew the picture in sharper relief than other writers, but it was the same picture which he was drawing. Moreover, the fact that he drew the picture in such bold strokes and that he pressed its implications home so firmly ensured not only that the conception was conveyed to the immediately ensuing generations but also that its inherent difficulties and limitations were obvious too. Thus, at this point, Cyprian's influence was open and consciously recognized; it was, therefore, followed not blindly but with critical awareness of what was being done. At this basic level, Augustine was able to combine respect for Cyprian's ideas with deliberate modification of their substance.

The same can be said of Cyprian's attitude to heretical baptism, which follows as a very natural corollary to his basic understanding of the nature of the church. In this also Cyprian was no innovator. His practice would appear to stand in direct continuation of the tradition embodied in a Council of Carthage under the leadership of Agrippinus, Bishop of Carthage, in the year AD 213. Moreover, the whole question was brought right out into the open both by the contemporary opposition of Stephen and by the subsequent controversy with Donatism. Here also, therefore, the influence of Cyprian was effectively controlled by the radical scrutiny given to his ideas in the immediately ensuing centuries of debate.

There are, however, other elements in the teaching of Cyprian, which were not so clearly formulated as conscious theological ideas in his own mind and which were not taken up in the same way in contemporary controversy or debate. It is at these points that Cyprian's influence upon us today, though less obvious, is liable to be more far-reaching. This applies particularly to Cyprian's ideas about the ministry and the eucharist, and I propose to survey these, briefly but critically, in the light of our understanding of Cyprian's personal and theological background.

1. The Ministry

Cyprian is by no means the first Christian writer to give to the ministry, and to the bishop in particular, a far more prominent role than it appears to receive in the New Testament. The names of Ignatius and Irenaeus spring at once to mind as earlier examples of a similar tendency. Nevertheless, Cyprian does represent an important stage in the development of the whole question of the relation of church and ministry whose significance must not be underestimated. In Ignatius we find great stress upon the necessity of obedience to the bishop as the focus of the church's unity; to do anything without the knowledge of the bishop is to render service to the devil. But, with Ignatius, there is no theoretical explanation of the bishop's authority given, no talk of episcopal or apostolic succession; the bishop's authority is simply asserted as the empirical answer to the threat to the church's unity occasioned by the heresy or heresies of the moment. Any deeper theological significance in the episcopal office is seen not in terms of succession but rather in terms of symbolic representation of the unitary authority of God. In Irenaeus the idea of a succession from the apostles does play a prominent part. But for Irenaeus the fundamental succession is that of the living tradition of the whole church, in which the succession of ἐπίσκοποι or πρεσβύτεροι plays a special part. They are seen as guardians of the church's public tradition, standing over against all Gnostic claims about the secret transmission of an esoteric tradition. The ministerial succession is one, admittedly very important, example of the total continuing stream of the public life of the church.

With Cyprian, the Ignatian and Irenaean emphases are combined and a significant new twist is given to the whole concept. In *Ep.*, xxvi. i Cyprian quotes the Petrine text of Matt. 16.18 and draws the following conclusion; 'Thence down the changes of years and successions, the appointment of bishops and the constitution of the church runs on, so that the church rests on the bishops and every act of the church is governed by these same rulers'. Here are the twin themes of obedience and succession. But most important is the reversal of roles as compared with the Irenaean picture. So far from the succession of bishops being grounded upon the succession of the church, it is the other way round; the succession of the church is grounded upon and constituted by the succession of bishops. The significance of this shift of emphasis introduced by Cyprian can hardly be overestimated. It has misled much subsequent Christian thought about the interrelations of church and ministry in a way from which we are only just beginning to emerge.

Hand in hand with this new emphasis upon the relation of church and ministry, there is to be found also in Cyprian a significant development in the understanding of the nature of the ministry itself. This development has frequently been studied, and my concern here is not to give any detailed descriptive account of what it amounts to, but rather to ask on what basis and for what reasons it makes its appearance in the works of Cyprian. In his famous essay on 'The Christian Ministry', Lightfoot speaks of a 'transition from the universal sacerdotalism of the New Testament to the particular sacerdotalism of a later age'. 'If Tertullian and Origen are still hovering on the border', he continues, 'Cyprian has boldly transferred himself into the new domain.'[6] With this judgment I would concur. Cyprian as usual is no radical innovator, but he makes the kind of development which, from one point of view may seem comparatively small, but which from another point of view can be seen as a vital step over the threshold into a new domain. Lightfoot goes on to ask whether the new more sacerdotal emphasis is to be traced to Jewish or Gentile influence. The question is an ex-tremely difficult one to answer. Lightfoot rightly dismisses the idea that it represents a straightforward continuation from early Judaistic Christianity. But that is not the only way in which Jewish influence could have been exerted. It is evident that Judaism, in a form that had more affinities with Palestine than Alexandria, was a considerable force in North Africa in the early centuries.[7] Cyprian himself came out of a heathen back-ground, but one of his earliest writings (or perhaps pieces of editing) took the form of testimonies for use against the Jews. I do not think we have the evidence to determine whether his heathen background or his sense of contrast with Judaism was the greater influence upon him in determining his great stress on the role of the Christian bishop as sacerdos. But one thing is abundantly clear. Whatever may have contributed to a sense of the need or desirability of some such development of ideas with regard to the Christian ministry, the means by which the new ideas were in fact presented and argued as Christian teaching stand out beyond mistake. The theological justification of Cyprian's idea of the ministry is solidly based upon a literal application of Old Testament texts concerning the Jewish priesthood to the Christian ministry. This point is not entirely new, but it deserves more emphasis than it normally receives.

In a recent paper,[8] Dr Hanson has studied Tertullian's inter-pretation of Scripture. He shows how Tertullian is far less liberal in his use of allegory than the majority of early Christian writers. In particular Tertullian solves the problem of Paul's attitude to the law by arguing that it is the ceremonial law only which is abrogated while the moral law stands still binding in its literal sense. But the difficulty of any such argument has always been that it is notoriously hard (I would say impossible) to draw a line between the moral and ceremonial portions of the law. In particular, as Dr Hanson points out, Tertullian appears to in-clude as something obviously binding upon the Christian the law against eating the flesh from which the blood has not been drained. Now Tertullian is the primary Christian influence upon Cyprian and it is clearly in this tradition of biblical inter- pretation that he stands. If the law against eating flesh from which the blood has not been drained is still binding upon the Christian, why not also many other injunctions of the Old Testament law, which might not (in our judgment at least) come obviously under the heading of moral injunctions? An example of this way of applying the injunctions of the Old Testament law, which clearly illustrates its essential arbitrari- ness, may be taken from Cyprian's own writings in relation to baptism. On the one hand, he can defend the practice of affusion on the strength of its use in certain purification rites ordered in Numbers 8 and 19.[9] On the other hand, he dismisses the argument that the practice of circumcising children on the eighth day has any relevance for baptismal practice on the ground that 'the figure ceased when the truth came and spiritual circumcision was given to us'.[10]

The connection of all this with Cyprian's ideas about the ministry is clearly shown by items 81–5 of the third book of *Testimonies against the Jews*. This third book is concerned more with the evidences for the Christian way of life than with anti- Judaic polemic in the narrower sense. The five items I have listed are as follows, a single text only being cited in evidence in each case.

81 That wages be paid quickly to the hireling.
   Evidence: Lev. 19.13.
82 That divination must not be used.
   Evidence: Deut. 18.10.
83 That a tuft of hair is not to be worn on the head.
   Evidence: Lev. 19.27.
84 That the beard must not be plucked.
   Evidence: Lev. 19.27.
85 That we must rise when a bishop or presbyter comes.
   Evidence: Lev. 19.32, 'Thou shalt rise up before the face

of the elder and honour the person of the presbyter (or old man)'.

This kind of reasoning about the Christian ministry is not something which occurred to Cyprian only when he was con-sciously engaged on the task of searching for testimony texts relevant to current Christian practice. It represents, rather, the fundamental ground upon which he bases his ideas about the ministry with unwavering regularity in the course of active debate. Thus, the obligation to appoint a bishop or priest in the presence of the congregation is derived from the method of the appointment of Eleazer as described in Numbers 20.25–26.[11] The illegality of a presbyter's acting as an executor is based upon the way in which the Levites were excluded from the perfor-mance of normal business.[12] The absolute necessity of obedience to the bishop is regularly asserted on the basis of the teaching of Deut. 17.12–13[13] and the example of Korah, Dathan and Abiram.[14] Finally, the invalidity, or rather the contaminating influence, of the ministrations of an unworthy priest is proclaimed as divine precept on the strength of the injunctions contained in Ex. 19.22; 28.43 and Lev. 21.17, 21.[15]

This last example will repay closer study, as throwing light upon Cyprian's methodology in this matter. His basic convic-tion was the unity of the church and the inconceivability of any form of salvation outside it. It was on this ground that his fundamental objection to any recognition of schismatic ministers was based. But Cyprian had also to deal with the question of priests or bishops who had compromised themselves in the matter of pagan sacrifice in the course of persecution. At heart his conviction was that such people had put themselves outside the church and needed to seek re-acceptance into its fold by penitence. Yet it is not on these grounds that he opposes the legitimacy of their continued ministrations. Instead, he employs the old law's insistence on the need for a priest to be without stain or blemish. This argument fits, as we have seen, naturally enough with his general understanding of the ministry as fulfilling the precise role laid down for the Old Testament priest-hood. But if the texts cited by Cyprian from Exodus and Leviticus are relevant at all to the question at issue, they are relevant not only to the particular case of a priest who has lapsed in persecution but to any form of impurity in the person of the priest. Thus Cyprian's argument, at this point, leads straight to the full Donatist position so vigorously combated by Augustine. As a result, this aspect of Cyprian's teaching has been entirely repudiated by the church in subsequent centuries. About that repudiation no regrets are required. The idea was, as we have seen, founded on a wholly unsatisfactory form of appeal to Old Testament authority. But what does need to be stressed is that very much more of Cyprian's view of the Christian ministry stands upon precisely the same foundation. Yet those other aspects of Cyprian's view of the ministry have been by no means so widely repudiated. Does not the whole conception stand or fall together?

2. The Eucharist

This aspect of Cyprian's teaching and influence can be dealt with much more briefly, both because we have far less direct treatment of the subject in Cyprian's writings and also because it is so very closely connected with the idea of the ministry that we have been discussing. This is not to say that Cyprian's influence is less important at this point; far from it. Just as in the case of the relation of church and bishop, so here also we find that Cyprian's teaching combines two already well-developed notions, but does so in a way which represents a radical change of emphasis of the highest significance.

In the rich and variegated thought of the earliest Christian writers about the eucharist, two themes stand out as of primary importance. These are the ideas of spiritual food and of sacrifice. Both ideas figure, for example, in the teaching of Justin, who is our fullest early witness upon the subject. In development of the first idea Justin can speak quite directly of the bread and wine

of the eucharist as the body and blood of Christ which we
receive for the nourishment of our spiritual lives.[16] With regard
to the idea of sacrifice, Justin (as so many of the early Christian
writers) quotes the famous saying of Malachi 1.10–11 about a
pure offering among the Gentiles as being fulfilled in the
Christian eucharist. Its character as a pure offering or sacrifice is
seen in two ways. On the one hand Justin agrees with Trypho
(and with many other of the most religious spirits of the age,
whether Gentile or Jewish) 'that prayers and thanksgivings,
when offered by worthy men, are the only perfect and well-
pleasing sacrifices to God'.[17] On the other hand, the bread and
the wine themselves can also be seen as the pure offering; they
are, in Irenaeus's words, the first-fruits of God's creation offered
back to him as a token of man's gratitude.[18]

It is these two ideas – the idea of the bread and wine as the
body and the blood of Christ by which we are fed and the idea
of the eucharist as a pure offering or sacrifice to God – which, in
Cyprian, are combined in such a way as to constitute a wholly
different conception of the nature of the eucharist. *Ep.* lxiii was
written by Cyprian to refute those who used water only (and not
wine) in the eucharistic cup. Cyprian uses the very natural argument that we should follow the example of Christ, but he
develops the argument in a very significant manner. 'It was the
wine', he argues, 'which Christ called his blood'. 'Therefore',
he goes on, 'it is apparent that the blood of Christ is not offered
if there be no wine in the cup'. Later on he puts his point
succinctly in this way: 'we ought to do nothing else than what
he did, for the Lord's passion is the sacrifice which we offer.'[19]
It is one thing to say, as did earlier writers, that the eucharist is
a sacrifice of thanksgiving to God and also to say that it is the
body and blood of Christ on which we feed. It is altogether
another thing to put them together, as Cyprian does, and to say
that in the eucharist we offer the body and blood of Christ as our
sacrifice. This is the step which Cyprian took, and it was fraught
with enormous consequences for the whole subsequent history
of the development of eucharistic doctrine.

If we ask, once again, what were the causes of this development in Cyprian's thought and what was its basis in his own
theological thinking, we have to admit that we have very little
evidence on which to go. But, since the idea of sacrifice belongs
so closely together with that of priesthood, it seems most reasonable to assume that they stand together in the thought of Cyprian
upon similar foundations. If that be so, we would have to say
that while the influence of current Jewish or pagan customs over
against which the church was standing may have had some part
to play, the primary influence is likely to have been the direct
application of Old Testament ideas to Christian practice. The
close relation of the two ideas of priesthood and sacrifice is well
illustrated by their proximity in the first book of the *Testimonies
against the Jews*. Items 16 and 17 read: 'That the old sacrifice
should be made void, and a new one should be celebrated', and
'That the old priesthood should cease, and a new priest should
come who should be for ever'. In the *Testimonies* the replacement
of the old priesthood is seen primarily in christological terms, as
fulfilled in Christ's exercise of the office of priesthood after the
order of Melchizedek. But we know that Cyprian also saw that
priesthood as very closely paralleled and fulfilled in the Christian
ministry. It seems likely, therefore, that he saw the Old Testament
sacrifices as fulfilled not only by Christ's sacrificial death upon
the cross but also by the sacrifice of the Christian eucharist.
Indeed, the wording of the rubric in the *Testimonies* – 'that the
old sacrifice should be made void and a new one celebrated' –
together with the quotation of the familiar proof-text (Malachi
1.10–11) in evidence is clear proof of the fact. There may well
have been a carry-over of pre-Christian ideas in the mind of
Cyprian, which made the idea of our offering the sacrifice of
Christ's body and blood a natural and palatable one for him to
develop and embrace. But it must surely have been in terms of
his particular understanding of the Old Testament that he
would have expressed a theological justification of his idea, if the
circumstances of the time had made any such justification
necessary.

The implications of this survey are clear enough. Cyprian had neither the opportunity nor the calling to be a theologian. The basic material of his thought was the common stock of Christian tradition. Some aspects of this tradition were brought out into the open as crucial issues of contemporary debate. On these Cyprian expressed himself with force. In these cases his ideas were in-fluential upon the later thought of the church, though by no means being treated as sacrosanct or beyond criticism. But there were other issues, with which this article has been more con-cerned, which were not to the same degree matters of public debate. In these Cyprian's influence has not been counteracted by the same measure of critical examination. Yet, when we look at his particular contribution to the development of these ideas, it is clear that it is of a kind which calls for very exacting scrutiny. The grounds and method of his theological reasoning are not of a kind to inspire confidence. Three features stand out in this respect. Most obviously and importantly, much in Cyprian's thought is based on (and not merely illustrated by) an approach to the Old Testament which is arbitrary and liable to minimize the distinctively new elements in Christian thought. Secondly, there is a tendency to combine elements of the earlier Christian tradition in a way which, while it obscures the novelty of what is being said, really represents a very significant development of ideas. Thirdly, there is the suspicion (though it is much more difficult to be sure on this point) of a carry-over of ideas from Cyprian's pre-Christian past without allowing for their radical transformation in the light of the gospel. Such characteristics are not surprising in a man obviously gifted with a retentive memory and rhetorical ability, but untrained and apparently uninterested in the realms of critical and philosophical thought. If my picture be in any measure a true one, it should serve to make the Cyprianic teaching about the ministry and the eucharist the more intelligible as a historical phenomenon; it should also, I would suggest, serve to make them the more open to question as theological foundation-stones of Western thought about these subjects – which to a great extent they still remain.

7

One Baptism for the Remission of Sins

The concept of faith as understood by some of the later writers of the New Testament and by the early Fathers is a pale shadow of that profound reality which played so large a role in the thought and writings of St Paul. If the nature of this defection has been not infrequently exaggerated by some writers, its substantial truth remains, I believe, undeniable. It has been less often emphasized that there is an almost equally important and not unconnected change in the understanding of baptism.

St Paul's teaching about baptism has been the subject of count‑less studies. While there is much in that teaching that still remains obscure and difficult, at its heart lies the idea of an identification with Christ in his death and resurrection. It is this element of personal identification with Christ that so largely drops out of the picture in the thought of the immediately succeeding generations. The more obvious but less profound imagery of baptism as a washing, which is already present in Paul as a subsidiary motif, becomes gradually the more dominant theme. A possible indica‑tion of this shift of importance can be glimpsed in the famous description of baptism as a 'washing of regeneration' in the Pastoral Epistles, where there is also a well‑known parallel shift in the understanding of faith. But it is in the second century that such changes are more clearly seen and their full implications begin to become more evident.

The most important of these implications concerns the problem

of post-baptismal sin. The new and un-Pauline, if extremely
natural emphasis upon baptism as washing raises acutely the
difficult question of sins committed after baptism. The obvious
suggestion of this simpler picture is that baptism represents a new
start, a wiping clean of the slate, a washing away of the stains of
the past. In other words it suggests that the significance of baptism is to be seen as retrospective only.[1] In, for example, the basic
and straightforward account of baptism given by Justin in his
first *Apology*, he describes its purpose as 'our obtaining remission of our former sins'.[2] Yet baptism was once for all and
unrepeatable; of that there was never any question. It is no doubt
true that there were, especially in Jewish-Christian circles at an
early stage, lesser lustrations practised within the life of the
church. But there is no evidence to suggest that these were ever
regarded as other than quite distinct from the one baptism of
Christian initiation. The grounding of baptism in the once for
all event of Christ's death would seem to have ensured that from
the start baptism also should be regarded as having the same once
for all, unrepeatable character.[3] Even those who, like Cyprian,
were at a later stage regarded by others as practising rebaptism
did not so see themselves; they regarded the schismatics or others
whom they baptized not as in need of rebaptism but as never
having been baptized at all; nobody ever used the phrase rebaptism to describe his own practice.

The difficulties arising from this view of baptism as both
exclusively retrospective and wholly unrepeatable are obvious.
Hermas gives expression to the problem when he cites with
approval the general position that 'there is no repentance save
that which took place when we went down into the water and
obtained remission of our former sins'.[4] Baptism becomes like an
ace in a no-trump hand – a vital card which it is dangerous to
play too soon.

The logical outcome of such tendencies would be to postpone
baptism until the moment of death, to delay the playing of the
ace until the last trick. The force of such reasoning was felt not
only by men like Constantine, the whole-hearted nature of

whose Christian allegiance might be called into question, but also by men as uncompromisingly Christian in their convictions as Tertullian. It is given characteristically pungent expression by him in his rhetorical inquiry why children should be rushed so hastily into the predicament of having used up their one chance of baptismal forgiveness before they have had time to sow their wild oats. A true understanding of the full implication of baptism would, he argues, lead men to fear its reception more than its delay.[5] But however strong the force of such arguments might be in isolation, they did not have the field to themselves. It was not solely a matter of the ever-present possibility of sudden death, though certainly the risk of 'going to bed with an ace' is one that has always to be remembered. More significantly two other issues closely affected baptismal practice. In the first place baptism signified not only forgiveness but also entry into the church; a church made up entirely of catechumens could hardly have been seriously contemplated. But also, even within the sphere of thought about forgiveness, other factors were at work. In the selfsame Tertullian who emphasized the dangers of early baptism the germ of the notion of original sin was taking hold, with its consequential suggestion of the desirability of practising baptism at the earliest possible moment.

So there was no easy answer to the problem of post-baptismal sin as posed by this stress upon the exclusively retrospective character of baptismal forgiveness. The safety-first policy of death-bed baptisms only, by which baptism would have been reduced to an automatic visa for entry into the heavenly realms, was never a solution which could have become the practice of the church as a whole. Yet the problem was an acute one which had to be tackled. In the Shepherd of Hermas we see what may be described as the simplest and most naïve attempt to deal with the question. Hermas could see that many in the Roman Church who had been baptized had subsequently lapsed and that pastoral concern demanded that something be done to restore them. With that oversimplified optimism characteristic of many a reformer he believed that what was needed was a new start and then all would be well. He did not, as we have already seen, question the rightness of the theory that 'there is no repentance save that which took place when we went down into the water and received remission of our former sins', but he asserted on the strength of a special revelation that there was to be one more chance for those who had fallen in the past. Just as the current baptismal theory allowed to the individual one occasion of for-giveness and after that expected no further lapses, so Hermas in the same spirit would allow to the church one occasion for receiving back the fallen and after that expected the old system of the one baptismal forgiveness alone to meet the needs of the church. But it was not to be. Saintliness is not to be secured as easily as that in the life either of the individual or of the church. Despite the prophetic utterances of Hermas the problem of post-baptismal sin remained. It was a permanent problem which could not be dealt with by *ad hoc* solutions of that kind.

The difficulty therefore could not be evaded. Baptism provided forgiveness of pre-baptismal sins; there must therefore be some other means of securing the forgiveness of post-baptismal sins. The problem is posed very clearly in these terms not only in the Western writers but with equal clarity by the great early Alex-andrians. Thus Clement of Alexandria writes 'Forgiveness of past sins, God gives; of future each one gives to himself',[6] and 'sins committed before baptism are remitted; those committed after baptism are purged'.[7] Origen in characteristic fashion finds a subtle scriptural basis for the distinction that he wishes to draw in Paul's citation of Ps. 32.1, 'Blessed is he whose iniquity is forgiven and whose sin is covered';[8] sins like fornication, he says, if committed before baptism can be simply forgiven where there is repentance; but if committed after baptism they cannot be so forgiven; they can only be covered.[9]

How then was such forgiveness which a man gives to himself, such covering of sin, to be effected? The simplest answer would seem to be that it comes through the conscientious performance of the duties of the Christian life. Hermas is told that 'if you will turn to the Lord with your whole heart, and work righteousness the remaining days of your life, and serve him rightly according to his will, he will give healing to your former sins'.[10] Cyprian speaks similarly of the lapsed as 'satisfying God with their prayers and works' and of 'constant and ceaseless labour, following the likeness of baptism, once again bestowing the mercy of God.'[11] Origen in a famous homily lists seven ways of sacrifice for sin open to those living under the new dispensation; these include various facets of Christian living (such as almsgiving, forgiveness of another, conversion of a sinner, an outpouring of love, or ecclesiastical penance) to which on the strength of some particular biblical text a propitiatory function could especially be ascribed.[12]

Within this whole range of Christian living which was believed to have the necessary sacrificial efficacy two particular activities stand out – the self-mortification embodied in ecclesiastical penance and almsgiving. No doubt both these, and particularly the former, were always regarded in part as tests of sincerity of the penitence being expressed. But it would appear that they were also regarded from the very start as having a more fundamental role to play. Hermas is told that it is quite wrong to think that the sins of the penitent are forgiven immediately; he must torture his own soul and suffer affliction, so that God may be moved with compassion and provide healing for his sin.[13] And Tertullian can speak of the penitential system of his day as 'standing in the stead of God's indignation' and as 'discharging eternal punishments'.[14] So also the propitiatory power of almsgiving is asserted by as early a writer as 2 Clement,[15] and in the works of Cyprian it figures with great frequency and emphasis. Not only is the theme developed at length in the treatise 'On Works and Alms' but it is also dealt with extensively in the first and longest section of the third book of *Testimonies*. And even in the heat of controversy with the rigorist Novatian, the mind of Cyprian moves naturally to the words of Tobit 4.10, 'Alms do deliver from death', as clear evidence of the legitimacy of restoring the lapsed.[16] So important did these distinct secondary

ways of forgiveness become that the words of the creed expressing
belief in the remission of sins, originally referring explicitly to
baptism, came later to be interpreted just as freely of such subsequent secondary means of forgiveness.[17]

One further factor needs to be borne in mind in seeking to
understand this development of a double standard of forgiveness.
The seriousness of a sin is commensurate with the clarity with
which its sinfulness was recognized in advance by the one
committing it. This principle is clearly enshrined in the words
of Luke 12.47, 48, to the effect that the servant who knew his
master's will and did not do it will be flogged more severely than
the one who did not know his master's will but did things
deserving a beating. Sins done in ignorance are not to be judged
as harshly as sins against the light. Now illumination is the
commonest of all early descriptions of baptism. Sins committed
before and after baptism could therefore be identified directly
with sins of ignorance and sins against the light respectively.
Such a distinction served to reinforce the kind of development
which we have been tracing. It made it seem not merely a matter
of practical necessity but a matter of moral appropriateness that
the way of forgiveness after baptism should be a more laborious
and painful one. Moreover this same distinction has less obvious
but not less serious implications for the understanding of baptismal forgiveness. If the forgiveness given in baptism is only for
sins past and those sins are to be distinguished from post-
baptismal sins in that they belong to the less serious category of
sins done in ignorance, it is no large step to suggest that the free
nature of baptismal forgiveness is possible because the sins that
it deals with belong to this lesser category. It is significant that
such ideas come to prominence once again in the later writings
of the New Testament and most notably in the assertion of the
Paul of the Pastorals that he received mercy because his past sins
had been committed ignorantly in unbelief.[18] This idea recurs
frequently in the writings of the second and third centuries.[19]
But if the free nature of baptismal forgiveness be thus grounded
in the less culpable character of the class of sins with which it

deals, then it is no longer being grounded absolutely in the free grace of God.

This whole course of development which I have outlined very briefly here is well enough known. Nor is it one which is diffi-cult to understand. My purpose in retracing it once again is to emphasize how immediate and how far-reaching are the conse-quences of an initial inadequacy in the understanding of baptism. That there are dangers of formalism and even of magic in the exercise of such an outward rite as baptism is well enough known. But the source of the difficulties with which we have been concerned here is of a less crudely obvious kind. It seems clear that if baptism be conceived as exclusively retrospective in character, then some development such as that which we have here described must ensue. It is significant that Newman should have chosen this as his one example of a case of development by 'logical sequence'. Starting from the view that the distinguishing gift of baptism as understood in the primitive church was 'plenary forgiveness of sins past', he goes on to demonstrate how the whole system of penance (and much more besides) follows on with inescapable logic.[20] The logical character of the development may readily be granted, but it can hardly be regarded as other than destructive of the truth of the gospel. Another Roman Catholic writer, d'Alès, following Bossuet, defends Cyprian against the criticism of Protestant theologians on the ground that he is not setting up almsgiving over against the blood of Christ as a source of forgiveness but that the true contrast is between the blood of Christ becoming effective through our baptism and the blood of Christ becoming effective through our almsgiving and good works.[21] But this line of defence will not do. It fails to allow for the fact that baptism has no other meaning than our identification with Christ in his death and resurrection. To speak therefore as if our almsgiving could be a second parallel means through which we receive effectively the blood of Christ is to treat baptism as if it were one of many good human activities and to miss altogether its true significance.

There is no escape from this dilemma except by denying

altogether that baptism ought to be regarded in this exclusively retrospective way. To do so does not involve repudiating completely the New Testament view of baptism. It does involve repudiating the second-century view and that of some of the later strands of New Testament thought. But it is in my judgment fully consonant with the Pauline view. John Knox in a recent book has criticized St Paul for preferring to think of God's act towards us as a justifying act rather than a forgiving act.[22] It is not difficult to sympathize with such criticisms. Yet this study has served to bring out some of the dangers that can arise from accepting too simply the thought of God's act towards us as one to be understood primarily in terms of forgiveness. Forgiveness most naturally suggests something which has only a negative significance in relation to the past. There may be overtones in the concept of justification which have their dangers, but there are also undertones in the concept of forgiveness which suggest that St Paul's relative neglect of so obvious an idea is not wholly to his discredit. Any categories to be used in the understanding of baptism must be essentially descriptive of the establishment of a continuing relation between persons. This is the great merit of the Pauline concept of justification when properly understood. It is the establishment by God of a true relationship between God and man by means of which the problem of man's sin as a barrier to that relationship is dealt with once for all. Its reference is not primarily temporal at all. It has that total timeless character which is implied by speaking of the eschatological nature of the New Testament gospel. If we are to spell out its meaning in temporal terms, we must do so in such a way that it has as direct a reference to the future as to the past. The concept of baptism as a washing away of past sins has an attractive simplicity about it, but let it once get a firm hold upon our thinking and immediately the problem of post-baptismal sin is on our hands. Moreover, that problem is of such a nature that it will demand that it be not left without some solution; yet posed in those terms the problem is insoluble except by dissolution of the gospel itself.

8

The Consequences of Modern Understanding of Reality for the Relevance and Authority of the Tradition of the Early Church in our Time

Two contributions are to be given under this title. No doubt they will be different. But will they be different because one is by an Anglican and one by a Lutheran? I can certainly think of other Anglican scholars whose treatment of the topic would differ radically from mine. Or will they be different because one is by an Englishman and one by a Swede? Certainly in thinking about these problems I am never conscious of thinking about them in a specifically Anglican way; but that is no guarantee that my Anglicanism may not be a very potent formative factor on my thinking nonetheless. I am more conscious of thinking about them as one directly influenced by contemporary English philosophy and culture. Confessional and regional differences cannot be wholly separated from one another, but I suspect that the latter is a more significant factor than the former at this point.

1. Modern Understanding of Reality

There is no one 'modern understanding of reality'. The variety and complexity of modern understandings needs to be stressed. If we restrict ourselves to the more highly educated sections of

Western Christendom, differing philosophical outlooks jostle with one another in calling for men's attention and allegiance. Perhaps 'jostle' is hardly the appropriate word, for existentialist and scientific rationalist approaches seem at times to lack even that measure of contact with one another which the word 'jostle' suggests. But it is not only a matter of competing philosophies existing side by side as a collection of alternative static entities. Modern concepts of reality are on the move; they change with ever-increasing rapidity. No sooner has a way of approach reached the measure of fixity requisite for conceptualizing and describing it than it is already being replaced as the basic outlook of the oncoming generation. Moreover is it justifiable to restrict our concern to the more highly educated sections of Western Christendom? Western technology has certainly produced a far more uniform approach to reality in the world at large than has been characteristic of earlier eras. But it has not swept the board entirely, and ought not to be treated as if it were without challenge or without alternatives.

Gross generalizations will therefore, as so often, be both inevitable and dangerous. It would be impossible (even if I were competent to undertake it) to discuss within a single essay the consequences of all the varying modern approaches to reality for our theme. And even if it could be done, because of its complexity it would be in danger of obscuring rather than bringing into clearer focus the things that are most relevant to our problem. I intend therefore to select boldly, but I hope not wholly arbitrarily, two outcomes of the Enlightenment which seem to me to differentiate modern approaches to reality from those of an earlier epoch. The two areas to which I want to call special attention are a changed understanding of revelation and the development of a historical consciousness. I recognize that they can be challenged as not modern (in the sense that their point of origin is to be seen more in the nineteenth than the twentieth century) nor universal (in the sense that at least in the form that I shall state them they would not necessarily commend themselves to every theologian). Nevertheless I judge them to embody an important shift in attitude from that which has been characteristic of human thought for by far the greater part of the Christian era. And while there will undoubtedly be even greater changes in human consciousness in the future, I do not think those changes will involve a going back from these insights to our older ways of thought.

(i) *A changed understanding of revelation*

Christians have not held to one uniform understanding of revelation throughout Christian history. Even in the West alone it has been an issue of debate between Protestant and Catholic and between Protestant and Protestant. But for all this variety of view there were certain underlying common assumptions within which all such debates took place. That common assumption could be expressed in some such terms as these. There is a way (indeed the only complete way) to the knowledge of religious truth which involves appealing to a revelation whose reliability is guaranteed to us by supernatural authority. There may be doubts and disputes about where that revelation is to be found or how it is to be interpreted. But the basic conception was not in dispute. There were certain places within the world of which it was both possible and proper to say: whatever this document or this person teaches contains religious truth; had it not been so taught we would have had no means of knowing it to be true, but since it has been so taught we can, without further investigation, be absolutely certain of its truth. This approach to revelation was primarily a matter of the generally accepted attitude to Scripture. It did not lead to a single firm unchallenged set of beliefs because of the notorious difficulties involved in reaching an agreed interpretation of Scripture. This difficulty had a very great effect in mitigating the outworking of the principle in practice; it does not affect the underlying principle itself.

An approach of this kind was characteristic of the Fathers and of the church as a whole down to about the end of the eighteenth century. There are still those who hold it today. Nevertheless in my judgment it has to be described as incompatible with the general trend of modern understandings of reality. That is not to say that the concept of revelation as such is no longer possible. It is rather a specific understanding of revelation that has become impossible for us. The specific understanding which is excluded is one which isolates a particular area of the world and claims that that limited area contains religious truth in a form which may require human interpretation but which ought to be regarded as immune from the kind of critical assessment which is free to question or challenge its truth. We are surely bound today to say that there is no area of human experience, however special its importance, however justly entitled to be called divine revelation, which can be allowed that kind of immunity.

This shift in our understanding of revelation is bound to make a considerable difference to our assessment of the tradition of the early church. It means that though we appeal to the same Scriptures, we do so in a significantly different way. It means also that our evaluation of the formal declarations of early councils has to be different from the evaluation given to them by many of the intervening generations in the continuing stream of the church's life. J. M. Creed writes of how 'a change in terminology corresponding to this change of attitude may be observed. In the nineteenth century it became less usual than it had been to speak of Christianity as "Revealed Religion", and commoner to speak of it as "a historical religion" or "the Historic Faith".'[1] That quotation serves to lead on to the second change in outlook which I want to stress before we take up the implications of these changes for our attitude to the early church in any detail.

(ii) A changed historical consciousness

Christianity has always had a more profound concern with history than most other religions. It has been concerned about the past because of its belief in the incarnation of the Son of God at a particular moment in the past; it has been concerned about the future because of the eschatological dimension in its faith. Indeed a case can be made out for saying that it is one of the parents – or at least the midwife – of modern historical consciousness. But if so it has certainly brought into the world an offspring which cannot but have a very profound influence on its under-standing of its own true nature.

What then is the essence of this changed historical conscious-ness? It can perhaps be expressed in some such terms as these. We are all today, in one degree or another, historical relativists. By that I mean that when we think and speak most carefully we recognize the need to assess all statements, especially statements of fundamental belief, in relation to the particular cultural situation of the time. This does not involve abandoning absolutely the categories of 'true' and 'false' in such cases; but it does involve abandoning the category of 'absolutely true' in such cases.

The Fathers, of course, were well aware of the limitations of human language for the task of theological discourse. They were never guilty of the error of believing that they were in a position to give precise or complete descriptions of the being and activity of God. Moreover they were fully conscious of the distorting effect that some philosophical approaches could have on theo-logical formulation. Such distortion was in their judgment one of the prime causes of heretical belief. Nevertheless for all that they did have a kind of ontological confidence, born of the prevalent Platonist outlook, that it was possible to make true (if inadequate) statements about the eternal realities of the divine realm. This philosophical confidence was further reinforced by their understanding of revelation of which we have already spoken. The phrase 'philosophia perennis' suggests the idea of a framework of ideas with a timelessness about it appropriate to its role of giving expression to timeless truths about a timeless God. N. P. Williams defined the 'philosophia perennis' as 'a synoptic science of reality which is capable of real progress and attaining to real knowledge, which, because it is rooted in the nature of things, whose author is God, must necessarily be harmonious with the revelation which proceeds from the same God' and goes on to speak of a theological tradition which believes it both possible and necessary to 'define the deposit of Faith in formula-tions ever more lucid and more precise, which because they are

utterances of a teaching "magisterium" which is the voice of the
Holy Spirit and are expressed in terms of the "philosophia
perennis" which is rooted in the nature of things, constitute as
close an approximation to absolute truth as is attainable under
the present conditions of human understanding.'[2] In the closing
decade of the nineteenth century Charles Gore could still speak
of Hellenism as having provided a 'language fitted, as none other
has ever been, to furnish an exact and permanent terminology
for doctrinal purposes.'[3]

Today it is surely impossible to continue such an approach.
Not only the categories in which we express our fundamental
beliefs but the form of the questions to which they are answers
are profoundly influenced by the rapidly changing cultural situation in which we live. This was true of the biblical writers; it
was true of the Fathers; it is true of ourselves. But the fact that we
are conscious of this influence in a way in which the great
majority of our predecessors have not been must involve our
holding an attitude to the early formulations of the Christian
tradition different from that which was natural through many
earlier centuries of Christian history.

2. Some General Implications of the Changed Approach

(i) Negative

1. Study of the Bible was one of the causes leading to the
development of critical historical scholarship and also one of the
areas most profoundly influenced and altered by it. More recently
the problems to which it has given rise have come to a focus in
the problem of the 'demythologizing' of the New Testament.
The most important insight of a typically modern approach to
the study of the New Testament is the recognition that the underlying picture of the world in terms of which all the writers operate
is vastly different from our own. This has led on to the conviction
that any worthwhile understanding of its message must involve a
penetration into the inner intention of that world-picture and
what is being affirmed in terms of it so that it can be grasped and

re-expressed in ways appropriate to our own day. All this is extremely familiar to us. But if such an approach is necessary in the case of the Bible, it is equally necessary in the case of the Fathers. Their world-view is not identical with ours any more than is that of the apostolic age. The need for 'demythologizing' in the case of the early church tradition may appear less imme-diately obvious because the Fathers write in a more philosophical and less vigorously pictorial vein than the New Testament writers. But this does not affect the basic principle involved. A comparison with the traditional use of language about God may help to underline the point. Some phrases, such as God's right hand, are so obviously pictorial that no one would dream of taking them literally. Others, such as God's fatherhood or crea-tive activity, can without much difficulty be seen to require an analogical understanding. It is less obvious, but none the less true, that to speak of God's wisdom, or even of God's existence, is no less analogical a form of speech. God is not wise nor does he exist in the finite way that we are and of which alone we can speak directly. So the fact that the Fathers express what they have to say in a comparatively formal and philosophical way should not blind us to the fact that it embodies a conceptuality very different from our own which cannot be taken over without a process of very far-reaching transformation.

2. It is often claimed that the issues raised by the Fathers are issues of fundamental and perennial concern to Christian faith. The claim is just. For the fundamental question with which they were grappling was the question: what sort of God do we believe in in the light of the coming of Jesus Christ? This issue is certainly no less fundamental today. Nevertheless alongside that claim must be set with equal firmness a necessary qualifica-tion, namely that the precise way in which those issues were raised then is always subtly but significantly different from the way in which they have to be raised today. I recall hearing Dr Chadwick begin a course of lectures on the Arian contro-versy by saying he was confident that there were no Arians present and equally confident that there were no Athanasians

either since none of us today shared the presuppositions which they held in common and which made the dispute between them possible. It was not simply a question of there being no exponents of a substance philosophy present; there may well have been. It was rather a question of no one sharing the more complex conception of a hierarchy of levels of being, without which the Arian position cannot even be formulated.

3. The task of theology as envisaged by the Fathers could not unfairly be described as discovering 'the meaning' of the Scriptures. In this moreover they were at one with the principal heretics. This description of their understanding of theology would require some qualification in a fuller account, but as a generalization I believe it to be not unfair. They were of course fully aware of the need for careful interpretation and of the difficulties inherent in that process. But they did believe that when that task had been done, the doctrinal beliefs which they affirmed constituted the true meaning of Scripture.

It is true that some theologians do still talk at times of all doctrine being in the end exegesis, so that when you have correctly performed the hermeneutical task you then have the full account of Christian doctrine which ought to be believed. But this seems to me to be an untenable position. It appears to me to be either plainly false or else to be a very misleading way of expressing a possible position. In the first place it is called in question by the historical issue of the canon. A historical approach cannot avoid being aware of the ultimately arbitrary nature of the division between what is just included and what is just excluded by the boundary-line between canonical and uncanonical books. In the second place the hermeneutical method involved is often so indirect that it becomes very difficult to claim that the final outcome of it has in any recognizable sense provided us with 'the meaning' of Scripture. The interpretative method has itself become a contributory source of doctrine in its own right and ought to be acknowledged as such. Finally even when we have completed the exegetical task, we have often on other grounds to decide whether what Scripture says is true doctrine or not. In this we see our task in a very different way from that in which the Fathers saw theirs. And we are bound to take this difference in our conceptions of the theological task into account in considering what relevance or authority their teaching has for us today.

4. The tradition of the early church has often been seen as a prism through which the message of Scripture can be seen in its true colours. Where Scripture by itself has an openness, an ambiguity about it, potentially capable of being read in differing ways, the Fathers, it is often said, provide us with the true perspective from which to read it aright. Their work can hardly fulfil that role unless it embodies a more unified outlook than characterizes the Scriptures themselves. To this end much has been made traditionally of the *consensus patrum* and of the decisions of the councils in particular. Earlier ages have not been unaware of some of the difficulties posed by differences between differing Fathers of the church, but for the most part these have been played down if not altogether overlooked. It is hardly possible to do so today. Just as we are more aware today of the diversity of Scripture than most earlier ages, so we are far more aware of diversity both of belief and practice in the life of the early church. 'Consensus patrum' is bound to appear today a less substantial and less workable concept than has often been the case in the past.

Historical study also serves to bring out more clearly the political, ecclesiastical and psychological pressures that helped to produce the decisions of the ecumenical councils. This again is not something wholly new. These factors have been recognized in the past and they do not of themselves automatically undermine the authority of those councils. Nevertheless they cannot help but reinforce our sense of the temporally conditioned character of the councils and thereby at the very least raise doubts about some forms of the affirmation of their authority.

But there is a much more fundamental question about the authority of the councils to be raised. That is the question whether it is consistent with our modern understanding of the way to knowledge to give unchallengeable authority to *any* conciliar statements, however impeccable may have been the manner of their original determination. Dogmatic utterances emerge out of the broader theological debates of their own time and it is in that context that they have their meaning. They cannot simply be taken straight out of their original setting and transplanted into the very different soil of modern theological affirmation. Yet it is in this kind of way that they have too often been used. They have been seen as a way of escape fromt he uncertainties raised by the variety and ambiguity of Scripture, and more recently by the work of biblical criticism. But such a use of them is essentially unhistorical and seems to me to be ruled out in principle for our modern historical consciousness.

It has been argued that the collapse of the idea of the infallibi-lity of Scripture makes it imperative to give to conciliar decisions a more absolute authority than has been normal in Protestantism. But this would be to act as if one could make up the breaches caused by modern approaches to knowledge in one sector of theology by redoubling the old methods of approach in another sector. It cannot be done. The posing of the problem is impor-tant; the conclusion must be the reverse. The true implications of the change in our approach to Scripture is the need for a parallel change in our approach to the Fathers and to the councils.

(ii) Positive

The implications of a modern approach with which I have been concerned so far have been largely of a negative kind. But it would be somewhat ironic if the development of the historical consciousness had exclusively negative implications for assessing the relevance of past history. It insists on understanding the past as the past and will not allow it to be transported, as if by some magic time machine, into the present. There are, it is true, those who would argue that what I have just spoken of as ironical is none the less true and that the implications of the modern his-torical consciousness are wholly of this negative kind. It shuts up each period, it might be claimed, so exclusively within its own particular time and culture that the relevance of the past becomes of negligible importance. I do not believe that this very widespread disenchantment with the past is justified or can be for long sustained. A historical approach has positive implications also. It insists that the present cannot properly be understood without reference to its past. An attempt to understand how we have emerged from the past and reached the position in which we now stand is a part of the process of interpreting our present situation. In terms of theology this means that without a knowledge of church history intelligent theology is an impossibility.

The negative aspect can be summarized in this way. Just as a theologian who asserts 'the Bible says ...' as if that settled the matter is not doing theology as it has to be done today, no more is a theologian who asserts 'the Fathers have said ...' or 'the early councils decreed ...' as if such an assertion could be of final and decisive significance. But the other side of the coin must be stressed with an equal firmness. A theologian who sets out to tackle the age-old problems of theology as if they were being raised for the first time today is equally unhelpful. Far too high a proportion of recent 'radical' theology falls into that category. It is rightly aware that theological judgments cannot simply be taken over from the past and treated as if they were our own judgments. It goes wrong when it implies that the form of the modern question can be fully understood, let alone answered, without reference to the way in which the same basic questions and earlier answers to them have become an integral part of the heritage in which we stand. One cannot treat the Bible historically and then apply it to our present day situation as if the intervening period of history were of no significance. A historical approach to the Bible necessarily entails a concern with the course of history that joins the apostolic age to our own.

The church cannot therefore ignore any aspect of its past; theology must be concerned with church history as a whole. But there are good grounds for claiming that within that whole spectrum a knowledge of the Fathers may rightly claim a place of special importance. Coming first in time they raise many of the most fundamental questions about the faith with which the church must concern itself in every generation. Moreover because those questions are being raised for the first time and without a millennium of Christianized philosophizing behind them, there is a freshness and a vigour about the way in which they are raised which even the Reformation cannot always match. It has often been held against the Fathers that they were involved in a pro- cess of 'hellenizing' the gospel and that that fact reduces the measure of their authority or relevance for us because it auto- matically introduces into the whole fabric of their thought a dilution or distortion of the true gospel. That they were indeed involved in the process of translating the faith from one cultural milieu into another is not to be denied. But that fact should not be seen as a detraction from their value to us; rather it is an enhancement of it. For we are involved in the same problem. It may well be that it is precisely from such eras of cultural transi- tion that we can learn most about the real nature of the faith.

Finally it should be added that the work of the Fathers em- bodies to a peculiar degree an integration of devotion and of reason. Both are essential ingredients of a living theology. It is not easy to hold them together in the modern world. It is not to be claimed that we could or should hold them together in precisely the way in which the Fathers did. But a theology in which they were held together in so thoroughgoing a manner is one to which we ought to be the more ready to listen with care and attention.

3. Illustrations in Terms of Particular Doctrines

The position we have reached so far is one which claims a relevance for the work of the Fathers to our own time, but which also stresses that that relevance can only be of an indirect kind. Even where our problem is at heart the same problem (and not infrequently it is) the form of the problem is always crucially different. In very general terms, they think of an eternal, spiritual realm about which, on the basis of the revelation given us in Christ, we can be led to make true and unshakable affirmations. A modern approach has to tread a different path, because it conceives its object differently. We must now try to illustrate this indirect style of relevance, this subtle intermingling of essential identity and crucial difference, with the help of specific examples.

(i) The Trinity

No one could be more sensitively aware of the mystery of the Godhead and the inadequacy of all human talk about God than were the Cappadocian Fathers. They never underestimated either the intellectual complexity or the devotional character of the work of theology. It is this basic characteristic of their approach which gives to their theology much of its enduring value. Yet it was these same Cappadocian Fathers who produced for the first time a confident and firmly structured account of trinitarian doctrine which has remained in all essentials the accepted account of that doctrine in the church at large down to our own day. The story of how they came to affirm the doctrine in the form in which they did has often been recounted. It seems to me that they were enabled to effect this remarkable achievement in religious thought for two main reasons. On the one hand they believed that God had revealed himself in a very direct and precise way in the text of the Scriptures. And secondly they believed that on the basis of this revelation and of the God-controlled use of human reason it was possible to make affirmations about the nature of God as he is eternally in his own being. Only on the basis of two such presuppositions could they claim that we can have reliable knowledge of the distinct persons of the Godhead, even though those distinctions belong only to the interior life of the Godhead itself and do not impinge directly on God's out-going activity which is always the work of the full triune Godhead. In other words they were enabled to reach their very impressive doctrine of the Trinity on the basis of a view of revelation and of the possibility of knowledge of the divine realm of precisely the kind which I have been arguing is incompatible with our modern understandings of reality. More-over it needs to be emphasized that these assumptions were not merely the particular form in which their views happened to be clothed; they were a necessary precondition of that particular development of the doctrine taking place at all.[4] Now if the doctrine is logically *dependent* on a view of revelation and of the knowledge of God which we cannot share, is it consistent for us to continue to assert that doctrine as firmly as the church, officially at least, still does? Does its formulation and devotional importance in the life of the early church provide it with an authority which requires us to continue to affirm it as the church's doctrine? Or may we not rather have to say that since we have to approach the whole matter of the knowledge of religious truth in so different a way, the nature of the belief that we profess at this point may have to be expressed in very different terms?

(ii) The Ministry

An authoritative appeal to the tradition of the early church has never been confined exclusively to matters of doctrine. It has extended also to the area of practice which neither can nor should be separated off from questions of doctrine. On no issue has the appeal been made in more determined or more varied ways than on the question of the ministry. The historical papers in this collection provide clear testimony to that well-known fact. Contestants have normally adopted one of two clearly opposed positions. The history of the early church reveals beyond serious dispute the early and widespread emergence of an episco-pal order of ministry. Just how early and how widespread have admittedly been matters of debate. Moreover modern historical scholarship makes us increasingly aware of the complexity and variety to be found within the story of that emergence. But the main fact of the emergence itself remains. And once the general character of the development has been admitted, it has normally been felt that two contrasting attitudes towards it are open. Some have claimed it to be a true development, desired and intended by God, which therefore remains binding on the church of succeeding ages – even though the exact degree of stringency involved might be regarded as open to variety of judgment. Others have claimed (as has been done even more frequently with regard to the Papacy) that it represents a false line of development with no relevance or authority for the church today, unless it be by way of warning.

There have of course been many refinements and variations in between the two positions so briefly stated here. But if these two positions do represent in broad outline the main alternative types of response to the records of Christian ministry in the early church, anyone strongly influenced by modern historical con׳sciousness must find the way in which the dichotomy is posed wholly unnecessary. I have been arguing that we need to see the early development of the doctrine of the Trinity as historically conditioned by the contemporary understanding of revelation and of religious knowledge. That kind of historical conditioning is likely to apply still more directly and more forcibly to matters of church order. The church (whatever else it may also be) is a human institution whose form and structure is bound to be affected by the forms and structures of the society within which it is set. This is not only inevitable but proper. If the church is to function effectively within society its form and structure must be determined by an interaction between the gospel and the world to which that gospel is directed at any time. Only if the structure of the church were conceived of as determined by the gospel alone, as corresponding to some timeless ideal form of the church, could the early church tradition be regarded as in any direct way authoritative in this area. This is not to argue that theological considerations have no part to play in relation to the Christian ministry; it is to claim that they can only play that part in relation to particular changing historical circumstances. The approach suggested would not remove questions of the ministry altogether from the arena of inter׳church debate. If accepted, it would make it possible to approach them in a far more flexible manner than has been characteristic of the churches in the past and is still characteristic today.

(iii) Christology

In this third example I want to put forward a more tentative and more radical suggestion. In the examples given so far, I have taken two obvious illustrations from the realms of early Christian thought and practice. I have suggested that we may have to find very different forms of words for expressing the kind of convic‑ tion that the Fathers wanted to express because of our different approach to religious knowledge and that we may have to con‑ sider the appropriateness of very different forms of order in the life of the church because of the different nature of the society in which we live. But in both cases I have taken up a generally positive attitude to what they were attempting to do and to what they achieved in their own time, while stressing very strongly the need for a thoroughgoing reformulation or revision of their specific affirmations and practices today. This might suggest that where at least we can find a substantial 'consensus patrum', there we can be assured of a firm and unquestioned starting‑point for our own theological work. This indeed is very widely assumed to be the case. Some words of Karl Rahner about the nature of the contemporary task in christology are a typical example. 'The most urgent task of a contemporary Christology,' he writes, 'is to formulate the Church's dogma – "God became man and that God‑made‑man is the individual Jesus Christ" – in such a way that the true meaning of these statements can be understood, and all traces of a mythology impossible to accept nowadays is excluded.'[5]

Such a statement, I suspect, would meet with widespread assent. Some might even regard it as rather bold and even dangerous. But what I want to raise here very tentatively is whether it is bold enough. Could it not be claimed that to treat the church's dogma in this form as the starting‑point of our theological reflection may be to allow a greater authority to the judgment of the early church than we are justified in giving to it? Many people today would admit to grave difficulty in giving sense to the church's specific affirmations about the God‑man in the traditional language of the two natures. Can we, while admitting such a measure of perplexity about the form, be absolutely confident about the rightness of the substance to which it was intended to give expression? I am not saying that the church was wrong in this matter, but I am asking whether this is not a question that the church has to ask in a genuinely open fashion today. Even where the mind of the early church can be identified as having a common direction and intention, are that direction and that intention automatically binding on the church today? I believe that question has to be asked and I have deliberately chosen to ask it on a matter of central importance to faith to show how farreaching its implications are.

4. The Problem of Identity

The kind of question that I have been asking raises in an acute form the problem of identity. By what criteria are we to judge if we stand in a true succession to the church of earlier generations? Even if we confine ourselves to the widely accepted position of my earlier examples with their stress on the need for a thoroughgoing recasting of earlier forms of expression of belief, how are we to judge whether that work of reformulating is being properly accomplished? The reexpression of fundamental beliefs is not like the translation of simple sentences from an elementary primer into another language. There is no straightforward oneone correspondence between the old form and the new. The reformulation cannot say precisely the same thing as the old formulation. There is bound therefore to be an element of intuitive judgment in assessing its adequacy or otherwise, which cannot be settled by any clearly prescribed procedure. It must readily be acknowledged that some claimed reformulations may in reality be contradictory to the gospel. It does not, however, follow from that fact that there must be definite and identifiable ways of determining which reformulations fall into that category and at just what point they do so.

If the implications of my third example were to be accepted and we are prepared to say that in some of their most widely held and fundamental convictions the patristic age may have been mistaken, the problem becomes even more acute. It does not imply that we should (even if we could) forget about the judg/ ments of the early church or seek to begin all over again. It does imply that we cannot isolate any particular element within the early church tradition as something that cannot be called into question. Our conviction that the Holy Spirit has guided and does guide the church cannot be used to rule out in advance the propriety of questioning and, if judged necessary, abandon/ ing any specific belief or practice of the early church.

This problem is not wholly new. In varying form it has been with the church all down the ages. More recently the church has had to face essentially the same problem in repudiating in prac/ tice the early church's understanding of Scripture at the behest of a modern approach to knowledge. It has survived the element of discontinuity involved in so doing, not without difficulty but certainly without the disasters foreseen by some. Our present difficulties are both parallel to the problem of a changed attitude to Scripture and an inevitable corollary of it.

What then can be said positively about possible criteria of identity? This problem has to be faced, even though it may need to be recognized in the end that it is incapable in principle of any clear cut line of solution. I have argued that the test of identity cannot be located in any specific isolable elements of Christian belief or practice. We cannot say in advance of any particular tenet that it is and always will be a test of the true church. This is not to say that the concept of identity through change is simply be/ ing abandoned. Continuity can be expressed not only by the con/ tinued presence of specific elements; it can also be expressed by a kind of family likeness which may persist even where there is change in respect of each individual item involved. It is surely identity of this kind for which we should look in the life of the church. It will be difficult to know when we have it and impos/ sible to be certain. But is it not the kind of continuity and iden/ tity that is appropriate to the realm of the Spirit?

In conclusion therefore I suggest that the tradition of the early church remains relevant to us today. It has still a role to play, though it will be a much more indirect role than has often been claimed for it in the past. It can never play a directly decisive part in what must be the increasingly complex task of determining contemporary belief and practice. I would be hesitant to speak in terms of its 'authority', though anything that has a role to play in determining what we say or do is entitled to be described as in some sense an 'authority' for us.

9

The Unassumed is the Unhealed

The history of doctrine is an important field of study. So also is the study of doctrine itself. Like the two natures of Christ they ought neither to be confused nor separated. 'The unassumed is the unhealed' is a phrase justly famed in doctrinal history. It is a question worth asking whether it merits a position of similar importance in the study of doctrine itself.

The phrase comes from Gregory Nazianzen's *Epistle* 101 and sums up an important aspect of his case against Apollinarius. It helps to show the vital religious concern lying behind the early christological debates. Also – and very largely for that reason – it was influential in determining the actual decision of the church to affirm the full humanity of Christ along with his full divinity, despite all the intellectual and other difficulties involved. Look-ing back in retrospect over the whole development of patristic christology, this firm insistence on Christ's full humanity is perhaps one of its most noteworthy features, and we are here given a glimpse of its deep religious roots. Thus the historical importance of the saying cannot be denied. But we need to go on and ask what validity, if any, it has for us as a continuing theological principle now.

The fact that it was historically influential and that it has an obvious religious depth does not guarantee that it has such valid-ity; all it can do is to suggest to us that the principle is one which merits – I would even say demands – the most careful and thorough examination from the contemporary theologian. It is this therefore that I want to attempt. What force has this phrase as a theological principle for us now within the context of belief in the incarnation? While this will involve a certain amount of historical reference by way of illustration and of the probing of possible implications of the phrase, the essential object of the enquiry is theological rather than historical.

Τὸ γὰρ ἀπρόσληπτον ἀθεράπευτον. What is the logic of such a phrase? Let us attempt first a minimal interpretation. It might appear that the words need be no more than a simple factual statement of the coincidence of two spheres of occurrence. We might (it could be suggested on this interpretation) already know that the divine Son has assumed a complete humanity and also already know that complete humanity has been healed, and from these two pieces of knowledge deduce as an empirical conclusion a coincidence between the two spheres of the assumed and the healed. In fact, of course, on the basis of such a theory we could only deduce that the assumed is the healed, which is not exactly the same thing as the *un*assumed is the *un*healed. We could hardly claim to have observed such a negative correlation as a matter of empirical fact – to have observed e.g. that the divine did *not* assume angelic nature or animal nature and also to have observed that neither angels nor animals have been healed – and from these observations to have reached the conclusion that the unassumed is the unhealed. The negative form rules out any interpretation of the phrase as a mere statement of observed fact; it implies that we see some kind of *logical* connection between the two: our statement must be understood to affirm a relationship between the assuming and the healing, which is more than a bare observed fact, one, that is, which embodies some sort of organic interconnection between them.

The γάρ helps to reinforce this conviction, showing that an interpretation of this kind corresponds to its original and natural role in the context of incarnational faith. Whatever the basis for our claiming to know this principle (and to that we must come shortly), its natural role is as a premise in an argument enabling us to proceed from existing knowledge about what is assumed to new knowledge about what is healed or vice versa. If the principle is known to be true, it would enable anyone already convinced that the divine Son had assumed a complete humanity in the incarnation to conclude that complete humanity was healed – or more accurately that one essential precondition for the healing of humanity had been fulfilled, and it would enable anyone already convinced of the healing of the whole man to conclude that the divine Son must have assumed a whole man. In this second form, it will be noted, the deduction works more fully; it leads to a more definite and complete conclusion. And this is the original and more natural form for the argument to take. The logical connection is presumably that 'assuming' is a necessary causative factor in producing 'healing'; but in at least its initial employment in theology, the epistemological order was the other way round. It was rather the conviction of full salvation which came first and which (on the basis of this principle) led on to the conviction of the divine Son's assuming a full humanity.

It might be objected that the picture I have painted so far gives the impression that theological reasoning is of a much more deductive nature than is in fact the case. I would urge in reply that our principle has frequently been used in that kind of way in the past, and is sometimes still so used today. When some new form of christological interpretation is proposed, it is not uncommon to hear in the course of critical discussion some such retort as: 'That cannot be a true account because it would not show how Christ could be universal saviour.' Implicit somewhere in such a retort is often to be found some form of 'the unassumed is the unhealed' principle. And where it is claimed that an argument of this kind can be decisive against a proposed form of christological statement – i.e. because we know the principle to be true, we can know your proposed christological statement to be false – then it is being used in a strictly deductive way. Thus it seems to me that the principle has been and often is used deductively: whether it *ought* to be so used is another matter.

Nevertheless I don't want to press this line of defence. It is important to stress that theology can proceed in a rational manner; it is also important to be clear that proceeding in a rational manner does not necessarily mean proceeding by a series of deductive inferences. It might be truer to suggest that the theologian grasps the nature of the incarnation, the form of human salvation and the interrelation between them in a single intuitive act. What gives him conviction that his insight is valid is not absolute certainty about one feature of the picture in isolation, from which he can then move by logical steps to similar certainty about the other features, but rather the self-authenticating character of the whole, when seen as a whole. In that case the affirmation that 'the unassumed is the unhealed' would not be a premise used in the course of an argument from (*a*) to (*b*), but rather a description of the intuited relationship which gives coherence (and thereby increased conviction) to the theological vision as a whole. If we prefer an account of this kind as better describing the way in which we reach theological conviction, it is, I believe, still proper to ask: granted that this intuited relation between the nature of the incarnation and the form of our salvation does appeal to us, does seem to strengthen our conviction that the picture as a whole is a valid one, *ought* it to do so? Can we give any reasons (in the broadest sense of the word) *why* this relationship should seem to us to be proper and even in some sense necessary?

Karl Barth would, of course, challenge the propriety of these questions I am now raising. I confess to feeling comparatively unperturbed by that fact, but it is worth spending a moment to glance at the position which he adopts on this matter. In the *Church Dogmatics*,[1] Barth writes: 'As we reflect on the way He has actually opened up, we can say that if He wished to reveal himself, if He wished to be free for us, this very miracle had to take place, namely that without ceasing to be Himself He entered our sphere, assumed our nature. He had to if He wished to impart Himself to us, to become the Mediator of Himself to us.' In other words, in reflection upon the revelation as we have received it, Barth does claim to see a necessary connection of the kind with which we are concerned between the nature of the incarnation and the form of our salvation. But he is determined to insist that this 'necessity' exists only because God has so willed things. So seven pages later he writes: 'Here we must venture the dangerous statement that it might have pleased Him to reveal Himself after the fashion posited by the theory of ancient and modern Docetism or Ebionitism, which does not do justice to the witness of the New Testament, i.e. by some sort of abandonment or diminution of His divinity. Were that so, were the New Testament witness to run otherwise than it now does, then we should just have to regard as necessary a reality corresponding to such a witness in the New Testament and indeed to one of the above theories.' This appears to me to be a rather perverse way of saying that the kind of necessity, the kind of logical connection with which we are concerned, is one of which we become aware in the light of things as they actually are and as far as we can tell things might have been otherwise than they are: there is no purely ontological argument to the nature of the way of salvation. All this seems to me quite unexceptionable – even a valuable warning against any expectation that the logical connection which we are trying to explore will be of a very precise or formal kind. It does not, I think, do anything to rule out as improper our attempt to examine the nature of that 'necessity' of which Barth himself is fully prepared to speak. It does not seem to me to make sense to say that we are aware (by whatever means) of a divine 'necessity' to act in a particular kind of way for the objective of man's salvation and at the same time not be able to say anything about what kind of a 'necessity' it is and why we apprehend it as 'necessary'. In speaking of it as 'necessary' we certainly ought not to think of it as a kind of law external to God to which God has to bow; but for the word to have any point we must mean something more than that it is as a matter of fact how God has acted.

Let us then go back to our principle 'the unassumed is the unhealed' and ask how we might claim to know it to be true and in what sense we are to understand it in the context of incarnational faith.

'The unassumed is the unhealed.' The language is of course, in the broad sense of the term, analogical. 'The assuming' and the 'healing' to which it refers are not acts of precisely the same kind as the 'assuming' and the 'healing' referred to when the words are used in ordinary discourse dealing with everyday human affairs. If, therefore, we know or believe this principle to be true with respect to 'assuming' and 'healing' at a human level, we might *expect* it to hold also with respect to divine activity; we could not however be *sure* that it did nor would we be justified in treating it as an unchallengeable principle available for use in a strictly deductive argument, since it might be precisely a point at which the analogy did not hold. But do we in fact have even the prior knowledge of such a principle at the human level? The strictly literal sense underlying the second term – ἀθεράπευτον – is a medical one. Now medical analogies for salvation are very natural, very common and notoriously dangerous. φάρμακον ἀθανασίς is a vivid phrase and I would certainly want to defend Ignatius' right to use it, but it has obvious dangers of suggesting salvation by inoculation. Medical language in its basic sense tends to suggest bodily healing and is always therefore likely to suggest a somewhat automatic healing process. Psychiatric healing, of course, might suggest a rather different picture. Drawing upon analogies of a mental and not purely physical kind is not infrequently to be found in the patristic age. Origen, for example, tells Celsus that 'since the human race was mad, it had to be cured by methods which the Word saw to be beneficial to lunatics'.[2] That would seem to leave a good deal of scope – including, for Origen, God's telling lies and deceiving men for their own good.

But even at the level of bodily healing what makes for healing in one case may militate against it in another. One kind of wound needs to be kept open to let the poison out; another needs to be kept closed to keep the blood in; one kind of growth may require immediate surgery, which in another case would be disastrous, and so on. It would be difficult to find any general agreed medical principle as the analogue behind the conviction that 'the unassumed is the unhealed'. Athanasius says explicitly that the medical analogy is an inadequate one: Scripture, he says, speaks of Christ 'bearing' our sicknesses and uses the word βαστάζειν and not the more natural word θεραπεύειν because the latter would have suggested a more external kind of healing activity than is in fact involved in Christ's dealing with our sins.[3]

The metaphorical sense of 'healing' therefore has no particular significance for our phrase and was of no special importance even in its initial formulation. The metaphor was a dead one and the principle could have been expressed equally well in terms of some other image of salvation. In fact we have a similar statement from the other Gregory – of Nyssa – in terms of washing: 'It was in keeping with his intimate union with our nature that he should be united with us in all our characteristics. Those who wash off dirt from garments do not leave some of the stains and remove others. But, from top to bottom, they cleanse the whole garment of the stains, to give it a consistent character and a uniform brightness with the washing. It is the same with our human life, which from beginning to end and throughout was stained with sin. The cleansing power had to penetrate it entirely. One part could not be healed by cleansing while another was overlooked and left uncured. That is why . . . the power which amends our nature . . . had to touch the beginning and extend to the end, covering all that lies between'.[4] In other words: 'the unassumed is the uncleansed'. Or again, no one has pursued this kind of reasoning with more logical rigour than Anselm, and in his case it was in terms of the paying of a penalty. 'The unassumed is the unremitted.'

We are unlikely therefore to find much enlightenment by pursuing in detail any one of the various images of salvation – medical, juridical, sacrificial or what you will. Let us see, rather, whether we can reformulate our principle in more general terms which could be applied equally well to any model. Let us try out a formulation of this kind: 'you have to get hold of something before you can do anything effective about it'. A little later on in the same passage from which I quoted a moment ago,

Gregory of Nyssa seems to appeal to the principle in very much this form: 'A sick man cannot be healed unless the ailing part of him in particular receives the cure. If, then, the diseased member was on earth and the divine power, to preserve its own dignity, didn't come into contact with it, it . . . would not have benefited men.' But will this argument do? Even our reformulated principle isn't true in a literal sense. You don't have actually to grip something with your hand to do something with it. There is such a thing as action at a distance; getting hold of someone is, as often as not, done on the telephone. Yet Gregory's argument seems to require a very narrow sense of 'getting hold of': the divine power must 'come into contact with' (ἐφάπτομαι is the Greek word), actually take hold of man.

In order to reformulate our principle in a properly generalized form, will it not have to read: 'You can't do anything effective about something without entering into some sort of relation with it'? That seems to me to be a true principle of human experience, but as with most enunciations of principles which one is pretty confident are wholly true, one has an uneasy feeling that it is pretty platitudinous – if not actually tautologous – as well. Certainly it doesn't seem to help us much if we try to use it theologically. God is never out of relation with man, even sinful man; if man were totally unrelated to God, he would cease to exist. In the light of our principle in its fully generalized form, I think we have to say (in contradiction of Gregory of Nyssa) that God is always in contact with man (in the sense of being in relation to man) and is therefore always in a position to do something about man's condition, and nothing can be said *a priori* about the form that the divine action will need to take in order to be effective saving action.

Is there any alternative to a wholly negative conclusion of this kind? Are we forced to say that in the generalized form in which alone we can be sure of the truth of our principle it sheds no light on our understanding of the incarnation and of salvation? Perhaps we are. But I want to make one further attempt to reformulate the principle, in a form that is slightly more specific (even if still equally platitudinous) and which might still prove to be of some positive and constructive use. Let us consider the following: 'You can't do anything effective about something without entering into that kind of relationship with it which is appropriate to your intended objective.' If you want to enable someone to stand on his own feet, you can't do it by entering into that kind of relationship with him which is constituted by carry-ing him on your shoulders. This surely is in a generalized form the kind of thing that 'the unassumed is the unhealed' is intended to convey. 'Assumption' – i.e. the taking of a full human nature into hypostatic union – it is being claimed, is the kind of rela-tionship between God and human nature in Christ which is appropriate to the intended objective of man's healing.

But is it clear that this really is the case? It seems to me that reflection on our principle in this generalized form (the only form in which it appears to be both potentially interesting and self-evidently true) points in fact (if it points anywhere at all) in a strikingly different direction.

In order to develop this more positive aspect of the matter, two important issues need to be raised – so important indeed that they ought perhaps to have been raised earlier, except that one can't put everything in the first two paragraphs. The two issues are these. First: what is the relation of Christ's humanity to ours? Because an odd feature of our principle is that expanded it comes to read 'What is not assumed in Christ is not healed in us', which may seem less immediately convincing than it does in its more pithy and epigrammatic form. And secondly: what do we understand to be the nature of salvation? I argued earlier that the particular metaphor of 'healing' didn't appear to be especially significant for our saying. But we can hardly pursue the principle in the form in which I am now proposing it – namely 'you can't do anything effective about something without entering into that kind of relationship with it which is appropriate to your intended objective' – and ask what kind of relationship is 'appropriate' to God's intended objective of man's salvation, without consider-ing more carefully what we understand 'salvation' to be.

We must look therefore at each of these issues in turn. First: the relationship between Christ's humanity and ours. It certainly appears to me that our principle must have seemed much more convincing to people who thought naturally in terms of the Hebraic conception of a real solidarity of all mankind in Adam or who were thorough-going Platonists (I put that sentence in the past tense to show that I am doubtful whether there are any such people at least in the Western world today). If there is believed to be a single reality – humanity – so that both Christ and we share (albeit in different ways) in the same reality, the principle appears more plausible than if we do not hold such a belief. On a Platonist basis, for example, it is clearly the same thing, the one reality of human nature (more real than the imperfect embodiments of it in each one of us), that is being assumed and that is being healed. Now clearly there *is* something in common between all men, which we are indicating by our use of the words 'human nature', but I doubt if many people today can really visualize or express that which is common to mankind as a whole as strongly as our principle seems to require if it is to retain its verisimilitude. The implications of this point are closely linked with my second issue – what do we understand by salvation? This question is perhaps both more difficult and more crucial than might at first appear. A good deal more attention has been given in recent years to attempts to reformulate christology than to attempts to re-express what we mean by salvation. This may seem a natural enough procedure in view of the way in which modern historical knowledge has pressed the problem of the Jesus of History and the Christ of Faith so forcefully upon us. Nevertheless if the Fathers were in any way justified in seeing christological belief as grounded in and in large measure derived from soteriological conviction, it means that our way of going about things, which gives such priority of attention to christology, is in danger of proving both frustrating and unfruitful. But despite this lack of much recent critical examination of the concept of salvation, we must make some attempt to say what we understand by it. Obviously we can't express this without the use of some analogy, but I want to suggest an understanding of salvation as an unbreakable relationship of loving obedience to God for which the best (though still imperfect) analogy is that of personal relationship. Another rather different but closely allied aspect of the matter is brought into useful focus if we speak in Irenaean terms of salvation as the effective overcoming of those obstacles which prevent the attainment of the always intended goal of man's creation, namely his being made fully in the image and likeness of God. Clearly a good deal depends here on the kind of conception we have of the fall. If we have a picture, as did many of the Fathers, of the fall as representing the absolute failure of God's initial plan for mankind, it might be reasonable then, with them, to envisage a totally different method at work in God's subsequent redemptive activity. Athanasius is quite explicit on this point: 'Perhaps', he writes in *De Incarnatione* 14, 'one might say that the same means were open as before, for the Word of God to show forth the truth about the Father once more by means of the work of creation. But this was no longer a sure means. Quite the contrary: for men missed seeing this before, and have turned their eyes no longer upward but downward. Whence, naturally, willing to profit men, he sojourns here as man.' For Athanasius God's presence to mankind in Christ for the work of redemption must be of a totally different order from his already-proved-to-be-unavailing presence to mankind in the natural order of creation. But I don't think it necessarily involves any underestimation of the seriousness of sin to reject so sharp a two-stage picture of God's working in the world and to conceive of salvation rather as a single continuing creative process within which the life of Christ is a central and focal point. Now any Christian understanding of the divine purpose in the whole creative process must take seriously the fact of human freedom. Without claiming that thereby we have a full theodicy, a complete explanation of evil, it seems clearly necessary to affirm as a fundamental feature of God's purpose that God has set man at an epistemic distance from himself, so that man may grow in maturity and by free response be led to his intended goal of free loving obedience to God. These reflections seem to be pointing the way towards a conviction along the following lines. If it is possible to say anything at all about what would be the relationship of God to man in Christ, the focal point of the saving process, which would be appropriate to the intended goal of man's salvation, is it not most reasonable to suggest that it would need to be a relationship of the same kind as that to which man is ultimately to be brought? Must it not be a relationship which gives actual expression to the intended goal of man's creation and not a relationship of a distinct and higher order?

One particular way in which the formative patristic period thought about salvation has, I believe, often obscured the central issue here and must be dealt with before I try to press home where the argument seems to me to be leading. I have in mind the conception of man's goal as θεοποίησις. If this is the real nature of man's salvation, it certainly seems natural to say that for man to be healed (= divinized), man must first have been 'assumed' into special hypostatic relation with the Word and thereby divinized. But the parallelism is less real than it might appear from my formulation of it (which is of course not my formulation but a paraphrase of Athanasius and a good many others of the Fathers). The goal to which our human nature was to be brought on the basis of this understanding of man's destiny was never understood to be identical with that to which Christ's human nature was brought through the hypostatic union; we are not destined to enter into that same union with the Godhead which is indicated by speaking of Christ's manhood as 'assumed', as 'made one person with the Word' and 'taken up into the Godhead'. Divinization is not a way of speaking of human salvation which I would necessarily want to reject out of hand; but if it be thought to provide an understanding of salvation in terms of which it can be shown that a prior divinization of man by the assumption of manhood into a relationship with God of a distinct, hypostatic nature in Christ is a logically necessary first step, then I believe it is simply confusing the issue through the ambiguity of the word θεοποίησις. It does not, it seems to me, stand on any different footing in this matter from any of the other models of salvation – healing, cleansing, forgiveness, etc.

In brief, then, my point is this. If salvation is understood in terms of a free personal relationship of man to God, and Christ is the way to that salvation, I cannot see any grounds for affirming that the relationship of the divine and human in Christ must have been of a different order from that to which man is to be brought. Yet this is precisely what our principle has been generally understood to show – whether as logical premise in a deductive argument or as logical link in an intuited vision. 'The unassumed is the unhealed' has been taken to imply that for human salvation to be achieved there must have been an 'assuming' of manhood into Godhead, a union of the Word to man of a distinctive kind (this being the implication in the term 'assumed'). I can only say that it seems to me that if any principle of the kind I have been trying to examine can be used at all as a guide to proper thinking about the incarnation, it should rather lead us to expect the same kind of relationship between God and man in Christ as we anticipate to be the intended relationship in man's ultimate salvation. If so, then the principle would tend to lead away from an insistence on the radical difference between the God-man relationship in Christ and that appertaining in mankind in general, to lead away, that is to say, from what has been a central feature not only of patristic, but of all orthodox, incarnation theology.

Perhaps this is not so surprising as it sounds. The principle was first invoked by Tertullian against the Gnostics and then by Gregory against Apollinarius – invoked, that is to say, against those who were making the God-man relationship in Christ even more different from that to be found in ordinary human experience than were orthodox teachers. What I have been trying to do is to elucidate the drift, the direction of this particular principle. I have ventured to suggest that in stressing the abso-lutely unique character of the God-man relationship in Christ, orthodox incarnational theology has (unconsciously) been going against the leading of this principle. If I am right in that it follows that traditional theology has been wrong in some of its arguments (which is hardly a very startling conclusion); it does not necessarily follow that it was wrong in its conclusions. Obviously it is impossible to draw general conclusions from the examination of only one argument. There are other principles and other evidence that need to be taken into account as well in determining belief about the incarnation and they too will re-quire the same kind of rigorous examination that I have tried to apply in this one case. In sum, then, I do not regard this principle as one that is wholly mistaken in conception or totally without value in practice, but I want to raise the question whether it ought not to be understood as pointing in a rather different direction from that in which it has been generally taken to point.

10

Does Christology Rest on a Mistake?

So presumptuous a title calls for some justification. Christology has never ceased to puzzle and to perplex the minds of Christians from earliest times. It would be outrageous to assert that because something in the realm of theology remains mysterious it must for that reason alone be being misunderstood. Nevertheless modern historical thought has posed the problem of the intelligibility of traditional christology in a particularly acute way and this fact places an obligation upon Christians to ask once again whether it is unmistakably clear that their christological beliefs do represent the faithful response to a mystery and are not the outcome of some mistake.

I do not intend in this paper to discuss directly the historical evidence about Jesus himself. In any full treatment of christology such a discussion would be essential and fundamental. I can only state here somewhat dogmatically that that evidence by itself appears to me to be ambiguous and inconclusive. The New Testament certainly includes evidence that has not unreasonably led the church to its affirmation of Christ's consubstantial divinity, but it also seems to me to include evidence that remains very puzzling on an orthodox christological interpretation. If that is a sound judgment, then the interpretative context and the basic assumptions in the light of which that evidence has been understood will be matters of vital significance. It is with these that I am particularly concerned.

Certainly neither the life of Christ nor belief in him as incarnate Son of God are things that can be considered as if they
existed in a vacuum. The life of Jesus happened in a particular
historical context and to speak of him as Christ is already to
place him in a very specific context of historico-theological interpretation. Similarly belief in him as incarnate Son of God did
not arise as an isolated phenomenon; it developed in relation to
other specific theological beliefs. That pattern of beliefs could be
spelt out in various ways; one obvious and basic way of spelling
it out is to say that belief in the incarnation arose within the
complex of beliefs – creation, fall, redemption. When Jesus was
thought of as second Adam, this implied both that his work was
a continuation and completion of the work of creation and that
it was a reversal of the disaster of the fall. Irenaeus may stress one
aspect, Augustine another; but in the full tradition both ideas
are present. Moreover, this complex of beliefs is not merely a
wider setting into which belief in the incarnation had at some
later stage to be fitted. Rather it is the matrix within which the
earliest examples of mature christological reflection took their
origin. Evidence for that claim is provided not only by the
presence of the second Adam idea (already referred to) in
Romans and I Corinthians, but also by the Adam typology of
Philippians 2, the image concept of Colossians and the notion
of the Logos in the Johannine prologue. If then the doctrine of
the incarnation has been from its earliest origins so closely interwoven with the doctrines of creation and of the fall, it seems
sensible to reflect upon it in very close relationship with those
two other doctrines.

When one considers the history of these two doctrines – the
creation and the fall – a striking point of similarity between
them emerges. In both cases it was for a very long time felt that
a certain specific action in history was essential to the possibility
of affirming the doctrine, essential to its survival as a meaningful
theological doctrine at all. The actions involved were of a very
different kind – one divine, one human – so that discussion
of them needs to be developed separately; but the similarity

remains none the less and is a fact of considerable significance.

With regard to the doctrine of creation, there is no need to do more than to recall in briefest outline the response aroused by the development of evolutionary theory a hundred years ago. The difficulty felt was not simply that evolution contradicted the account of Genesis understood in a literal, fundamentalist sense. In a broader, more theological way it was felt by some to contradict the basic affirmation of God's creation of man in his own image. Many who accepted the general truth of evolutionary theory sought to maintain a place for the specific creative action of God in the gap between inorganic matter and life or in the gap between man as a rational being and irrational animals. A position of this general kind is still frequently affirmed in Roman Catholic teaching. Thus we can read for example in a recent dictionary of theology: 'We can say that from amoeba to physical man, as it were, the process of evolution was complete and continuous. God could have willed the process to stop there, but instead something new was created, something which was not part of the biological process occurred. Something was gratuitously *added* to the evolutionary process in that God created a human spiritual soul which had no biological connections with any organism previous to that which it now informed. . . .'[1] But very many Christians today would regard this kind of an approach, which looks for some specific creative act of God within the evolutionary process even though not as part of it, as a mistaken one. Those of us who do so ought to recognize that we do so not because we have evidence that can show it to be false, but because it embodies a method of reasoning with which we do not and cannot identify ourselves. Moreover the grounds of this objection are religious as much as scientific. Already in the nineteenth century, Aubrey Moore could write: 'Apart from the scientific evidence in favour of evolution, *as a theory* it is infinitely more Christian than the theory of "special creation" . . . *A theory of occasional intervention implies as its correlative a theory of ordinary absence.*'[2] In other words, whereas to some the idea of a specific divine act of the creation of man – or at least man's soul –

seemed essential to the doctrine of creation, to others it has come to seem not only unnecessary but even inimical.

Recent attitudes to the doctrine of the fall are, if anything, even more familiar. Denial of the historicity of the Adam story was seen by some as undermining an essential Christian doctrine. Here again this was not simply a matter of contradicting the Genesis story. The difficulty could also be felt in a more sophisticated way as for example in the defence of monogenism in *Humani Generis*, where it is affirmed that 'original sin is the result of a sin committed, in actual historical fact, by an individual man named Adam, and it is a quality native to all of us, only because it has been handed down by descent from him'. The reason given for this judgment is that no other view is compatible with the doctrine of original sin. But once again many Christians react very differently and are more likely to agree with J. S. Whale when he wrote: 'The Fall relates not to some datable aboriginal calamity in the historic past of humanity but to a dimension of human experience, which is always present – namely, that we who have been created for fellowship with God repudiate it continually; and that the whole of mankind does this along with us.'[3] Moreover so far from regarding such an interpretation as undermining the doctrine of the fall, they would be more likely to claim that it helps to rescue that doctrine from certain embarrassments (e.g. concerning the manner of the transmission of original sin) which belong to it in any form which stresses the historicity of Adam's primordial transgression.

In both these cases, then, we see a tendency to regard the doctrines concerned as logically tied to particular events. I believe that we now have grounds for claiming that the attitude was a mistaken one. This gives us no right to feel superior or scornful in relation to our predecessors on that score. Their attitude was not unreasonable. The doctrines do seem to lose something of their toughness, something of their cutting edge with the loosening of what was once thought to be a firm logical bond. Something of the direct divine element in the doctrine of creation does seem to go if we do not speak of any specific divine act within the process by which human existence was brought into being. Nevertheless I do think that the old view was mistaken; I do think that the untying of the old bond not only frees us from an embarrassment in relation to scientific thought but also enables us to affirm divine creation in a fuller and more transcendent sense as religious thought itself requires. Thus older forms of the doctrine of creation and of the fall did rest on a mistake – albeit a very respectable and not easily detectable mistake.

Now I have already argued that the doctrine of the incarnation arose in the closest conjunction with these two doctrines, both of which had this kind of mistake built into them. It does not therefore seem unreasonable to ask whether it also, in its tradi⟨ tional form, grew up with the same kind of mistake built into it. When we compare the doctrines in this way, the parallels are, I think, striking.

The first disciples and countless Christians down the ages have been convinced that through Christ the redeeming grace of God was at work; it was at work in a way which they could not describe in lesser terms than the crowning of God's creative work and the reversal of the fall. But how could that be? Creation was in a special sense God's act; the redemption which was the climax and the crown of that creation must be God's work in every bit as full a way. The fall was a single act with universal consequences for ill; as its reversal, Christ's redeeming act must embody an equally universal transformation of the human situation for righteousness. Divine action of a quite special kind must be embodied in Christ's person and in his saving activity. Only so could the redeeming grace of Christian experience be adequately accounted for. But we have seen that in spite of what might reasonably be anticipated, the doctrine of creation does *not* require the postulation of any specific divine act within the process as a whole; indeed such an act would be an embarrassment to the expression of that doctrine in its full transcendent reality. Can we not say the same of the doctrine of redemption? Is it perhaps possible that the truth of that doctrine would even stand out more clearly if it were not tied to one particular act or life differing in kind from the rest of the series of human acts and human lives? If the doctrine of the fall 'relates not to some datable aboriginal calamity in the historic past . . . but to a dimension of human experience', may not the same both negatively and positively be said of the doctrine of redemption?

The heart of the suggestion, therefore, that I want to put forward in this paper is that traditional christology rests on a mistake in this sense. It arose because it was not unnaturally, yet none the less mistakenly, felt that the full divine character of redemption in Christ could only be maintained if the person and act of the redeemer were understood to be divine in a direct and special sense. In the parallel cases of creation and fall our forefathers had to learn – and it was a painful process – that what they thought was a logically necessary link between the theological assertion and particular occurrences in history was not as logically necessary as they thought it to be. Are we perhaps at the equivalent – and even more painful – moment of learning the same truth about the doctrine of redemption?

That is the heart of what I want to suggest. But it seems appropriate to go on and give some brief indication of what more positive lines of thought might take the place of a traditional christological approach, if it were to be concluded that that did indeed rest on a mistake. And here too there is help to be found in a consideration of the doctrine of creation. If we do not accept the idea of a special act of creation at some point within the evolutionary process, in what sort of way do we give fuller expression to the doctrine? What do we say about it beyond a bald affirmation of God's creatorhood? It seems to me that what we do is to tell two different kinds of story. On the one hand we tell the scientific story of evolution; it is the real world as it has really developed with which the doctrine of creation is concerned, not with some ideal world of the theological imagination. But in addition we tell a frankly mythological story about the spirit of God moving on the face of the chaotic waters, about God taking the dust of the earth, making man in his own image, and breathing upon him so that he becomes a living soul. If we know what we are doing we can weave the two stories together in poetically creative ways – as indeed the poet combines logically disparate images into new and illuminating wholes. But we don't try to bind the two stories together at some specific point, claiming divine action to be at work in a special sense in the emergence of a first man with a distinct spiritual soul. Nevertheless, although we would regard it as falling back into the old mistake to isolate such a moment as different in kind from other moments in the process, we would still regard that aspect of the evolutionary story – the emergence of the distinctively human – as a part of the whole story which has special significance for the doctrine of creation. We have to be concerned with the whole story; we do not see that moment within the story as related in a different way to the divine or mythological story, but we still regard it as a part of the story which sheds a particular light on the significance of the story as a whole.

Can we not speak in a similar way of incarnation and redemption? Here too, I suggest, we will need to tell two stories. In the first place a human story of the partial overcoming in human lives of that repudiation of the fellowship with God of which the doctrine of the fall speaks. And also a mythological story of God's total self-giving, God's compassionate acceptance of pain and evil whereby that overcoming is made possible and effective. We may interweave these two stories in various ways; in the gospels themselves they are already so interwoven and for religious purposes we need to have it so. But we do not need – indeed on this analysis we would be wrong – to tie the two stories together by claiming that at one particular point, namely the life, death and resurrection of Jesus of Nazareth, the two stories are literally united with one another. Nevertheless it could still be reasonable to give to the life of Jesus a special place as illuminating, as no other life, the significance of the whole story, as bringing home to us effectively the transcendent divine truth which the mythological story in its own way is designed to proclaim.

The inevitable – and quite proper – question is why *this* story?

Why should the life of Jesus fulfil this role as no other life, if it is not united to the divine, mythological story in any distinctively different way? We are faced here once again with the apparent Achilles heel of all reductionist christologies. The traditional answers are familiar; we can speak of the perfect measure of his obedience to God, the creative character of his life as seen in the transformation of the disciples and the emergence of the church. But such answers, as we know, have always seemed to the majority of Christians to be inadequate, to leave unsaid the one thing needful. Is there any point then in trotting them out once again? Only this. It has been the burden of this paper to try to show how it might be that the church should have so persistently felt the need to say something more and yet have been mistaken in that persistent feeling. The theological conviction of the reality of divine redemption was felt to require the underpinning of a distinct divine presence in Jesus; but in the light of the comparison with other related doctrines it seems reasonable to suggest that that very natural feeling rests on a mistake. In that case the inadequacy of what I have called the reductionist accounts of the specialness of Jesus – though they certainly have their weaknesses and their problems – need not be as fundamental as has normally been assumed.

It would be premature to assess how such discussion of the specialness of Jesus might develop in detail if it were freed from the anxious concern to give an account of that something more which Christian consciousness has seemed to demand. The precise form of the answer to the question, 'Why *this* story?', would need to depend very largely on the context within which it was being raised. If it is raised in a specifically Christian context, where the alternative stories in mind as possible focal embodiments of the doctrine of redemption might be the stories of an Augustine or a Francis, it would be pertinent to point to the directness of the relation of Jesus to God in contrast to the mediatorial role of the person of Jesus himself in Augustine's and Francis's own understandings of their relationship with God. In other words the story of Jesus is not an arbitrarily chosen story;

from a Christian standpoint, it is the story of that historical happening which did in fact create a new and effective realization of divine redemption at work in the lives of men, and which has remained the inspirational centre of the community of faith to which we belong from that day until now. There are certainly grave problems concerned with how much we can know with confidence of that story in its original historic form and of how far we can enter into the very different thought-forms and assumptions of that earlier period. But I do not think that these difficulties need undermine the centrality of the story of Jesus for faith. The difficulties are just as real for an orthodox christology which takes seriously its affirmation of the humanity of Jesus.

If on the other hand the question is raised in an inter-religious context, as is bound increasingly to be the case, it raises further problems and will have to be approached in a very different way. In many discussions of basic issues there comes a point at which we reach a limit question, where we have to say 'I can give no further reasons for seeing the thing as I do; this is my vision; do you not feel drawn to share it too?' Two historians may agree on all critical questions in assessment of the available evidence on some issue, and yet tell the resultant historical story in very different terms. Two moralists may agree on the factual aspects of a particular situation and on the moral issues involved, and yet make divergent moral judgments on what ought to be done in the situation. Discussion of the facts of the case and of the relevant criteria is important and in many cases may lead one person or the other to revise his judgment; but there may come a point at which, having been through such a process, there are no more reasons to be given. Each can only commend his vision to the other. Something like this is true, I believe, with regard to the basic affirmation of theism. May it not be so with the Christian's understanding of the specialness of Christ? There are many things to be said which give grounds for seeing the life and death of Jesus as a part of the human story which is of unique significance in relation to seeing the human story as a whole as a true story of divine redemption at work. To ask for some further ontological justification of that vision would be to succumb to the category mistake of confusing the human historical story with the divine mythological story.

I began by acknowledging the presumptuous nature of the question embodied in the title of the paper; I must end by acknowledging the presumptuous nature of the answer embodied in the paper itself. That presumption may perhaps be mitigated somewhat by an insistence that the answer proposed is put forward tentatively as an intended stimulus to further discussion. But there is a kind of presumption of which it may be accused to which I would plead firmly not guilty. There are parallels between what I have been trying to say and what John Knox has written in his *Humanity and Divinity of Christ*. Dr Mascall has accused him in that book of 'dismissing ... the whole of the classical Christology from Athanasius and Cyril ... to Augustine and Aquinas and beyond' and of implying that 'the great thinkers of the Christian church' were 'incurably boneheaded'.[4] It is true that, if I am right, the whole of the classical christology would have to be dismissed as resting on a mistake – in the specific form in which it was undertaken though not in all the insights lying behind the attempt. But this, I would insist, does not imply in any way at all that those early thinkers were 'incurably boneheaded', any more than to deny the inerrancy of Scripture involves passing an unfavourable judgment on the intelligence of those earlier generations who accepted it without question. What I have suggested may well be wrong; but I do not believe that it can rightly be dismissed on the basis of any claim that it would entail regarding all earlier christological discussion as a form of meaningless gibberish or all earlier faith in the divinity of Christ as regrettable superstition. No such entailment is involved.

II

Religious Authority and Divine Action

'Begin at the beginning, and go on till you come to the end: and then stop.' The King of Hearts' advice is not as easy to follow as might seem on first hearing. It is not simply that I want to speak about the interrelation between two major subjects and there is a certain arbitrariness in choosing with which of the two to start. The problem is far more fundamental than that. Where for the theologian is 'the beginning'? At whatever point he does begin he is always uneasily aware that way back behind the point that he has chosen there probably lie a number of un-questioned assumptions which have largely prejudged the kind of answer he will give to the very question he is setting out to investigate. This difficulty is not, of course, peculiar to the theo-logian. None of us, whatever the subject of our investigation, can ever really 'begin at the beginning'. But if this is a difficulty which the Christian theologian shares with other scholars it is none the less real for that. One obvious and important feature of the tradition in which the Christian theologian stands is that it gives some kind of special authority to the Bible, to the church and above all – though it is sometimes a little bit elusive to know exactly what is meant by saying this – to Christ himself.

Now if we agree that the acceptance of some authority of this kind, even in the most general sense, is a part of the tradition within which a Christian theologian works, we shall have to acknowledge that when we take up the question of divine action, of what we can properly mean by speaking of God acting, we appear to be deeply committed already on the subject of our investigation – and that in a twofold manner.

In the first place, we are committed in what I would call a formal way by the bare fact that we do accept certain books or certain people as having special authority for us; there is, that is to say, an element of prejudgment in relation to our theme implicit in the mere fact of such an acceptance in itself quite apart from what the particular books or people in question may actually say. For whatever may be our precise conception of the inspiration of the prophets or biblical writers, whatever may be our precise understanding of the guidance by which church councils or the Magisterium reach their decisions, it has normally been understood to involve some kind of special divine action, action of a distinctive kind, in relation to those people or those occasions.

But we are also committed in a second way, in what I would call a substantial way, by the content of what those authorities do in fact say to us. This is very much more than a matter of the Bible being a book which includes a number of miracle stories. The idea of divine providential action seen in a series of specific historical events runs right through the Bible, so that a well-known book of biblical theology can very properly be entitled 'God who acts'.

Thus form and content serve to reinforce one another. Unless God acts in a special way in special events it is difficult to see how we could have religious authorities from within history with the degree of specialness which Christians do in fact ascribe to their authorities. And those very authorities in fact do speak of a God who acts in precisely that kind of a way. A Christian, therefore, it is widely felt, must accept a conception of God's acting in the world of this kind – or else, everything collapses; nothing would remain that could merit the title of being specifically Christian.

Now it seems to me that there are obvious difficulties in affirming this view of special divine actions in the world. A good many people, I would suggest, do feel misgivings about it but continue to affirm it nevertheless because they do not believe that it is possible to affirm a recognizably Christian faith on any other terms. The situation is similar to that by which many people have maintained – and indeed still do maintain – a near fundamentalist understanding of Scripture, despite being well aware of the grave difficulties inherent in that position, because they do not believe it is possible to affirm the Bible to be divine revelation in any serious sense on any other terms. It seems important therefore to ask whether this conception of divine action is as necessary to a recognizably Christian faith as on the face of it it appears to be.

The kind of misgiving to which I refer is I think clear enough but it can perhaps be made clearer by a comparison with the realm of science and the concept of God's action in the natural world. In the Newtonian system, as is well known, nature functioned for the most part as a self-regulating system, but certain special actions on the part of God were required to correct, for example, the irregularities caused by the mutual attraction of the planets. As further advances in knowledge made possible normal scientific explanations of these phenomena, so this 'God of the gaps' was edged further and further out of the world. This process has not meant, however, that it has become impossible to speak in any way at all of God in relation to the natural world. Rather, I would want to say, it has made possible the reaffirmation of a more profound concept of God as the transcendent ground of there being a world at all. Is there then any parallel in the historical field? Do traditional accounts of the Christian faith really involve a God of the historical gaps? And if so, would modification of that conception lead to the impossibility of affirming a recognizably Christian faith at all or might it lead to the possibility of reaffirming it in a more profound and more satisfactory form?

No one has been more acutely aware of this problem in our own time than Rudolf Bultmann. It is an essential part of that fundamental concern which gave rise to his programme of demythologization. Yet Bultmann insists most emphatically that the concept of God's decisive act in Jesus Christ must be maintained, for it is in his judgment the very heart of the Christian gospel. For this he has been vigorously attacked by many of his critics who have claimed, in the words of one of them, that 'these two words (act of God) set up a whole mythical universe'.[1] The criticism has been levelled from both sides. Some have seen in his insistence on the necessity to retain the idea of an 'act of God' a welcome victory of his Christian heart over his demythologiz/ ing head; they have regarded it as an arbitrary limit to his demythologizing programme imposed upon him by his Chris/ tian convictions but thereby calling in question the necessity and the validity of the earlier stages of his demythologizing. Others, from the more radical side, have seen in it a regrettable failure of nerve, an unjustifiable refusal to press through with his pro/ gramme of demythologizing to its logical and desirable con/ clusion. Bultmann has defended himself by claiming that the concept of an act of God as he understands it is not mythological at all but analogical. Whether or not that is a satisfactory terminological distinction is not a matter of great importance for us here; but the substantive content of the distinction he is trying to establish is of central importance to my present concern. This is how Bultmann himself makes the point in answering his critics:

Mythological thinking represents the divine action . . . as an action that breaks into and disrupts the continuum of natural, historical, or psychical events – in short, as a 'miracle'. In so doing it objectifies the divine action and projects it on to the plane of worldly occurrences. In truth, however, . . . an act of God is not visible to the objectifying eye and cannot be demonstrated in the manner of worldly events. The idea of unworldliness and transcendence of the divine action is only preserved when such action is represented not as something that takes place *between* worldly occurrences, but rather as something that takes place in them, so that the closed con/ tinuum of worldly events that presents itself to the objectifying eye remains untouched. God's act is hidden to every eye but that of faith. The only thing generally visible and demonstrable is the 'natural' occurrence. It is in it that God's hidden action takes place.

· · · · · ·

In faith the closed weft (of cause and effect) presented or produced by objective observation is transcended, though not as in mythological thought. For mythology imagines it to be torn asunder, whereas faith transcends it as a whole when it speaks of the activity of God.[2]

Now there are certainly many serious difficulties in what Bult- mann is trying to say here, but I do not think it is difficult to see the nature of the fundamental distinction he wants to make by which an 'act of God' is not a mythological concept in his sense. It is closely parallel to the familiar avoidance of a 'God of the gaps' approach to the natural world. Divine acts do not take place 'between worldly occurrences' – i.e. in the gaps left by natural events, but in them in a hidden manner which does not affect in any way the closed weft of cause and effect. Moreover this does not involve, for Bultmann, a weakening of the religious significance of the conception of God's activity in history; rather it makes possible its fully transcendent character.

If something of this kind is a fair account of what Bultmann intends when he speaks of an 'act of God', a number of impor- tant questions have to be faced. Is it a possible conception? or is it a muddled attempt to hold on to the old religious language while abandoning the religious reality which that language was designed to express? If it is a possible conception, are there grounds for affirming it to be true or at least worthy of belief? And, even if there are, can we claim that it does justice to the main traditional affirmations of the Christian faith?

It is easy to put the challenge that Bultmann's notion of an act of God is vacuous in a down to earth no-nonsense manner. In an article entitled 'Does the "God who acts" really act?'[3] an American writer, F. B. Dilley, argues that the biblical theo- logian must choose between acknowledging the reality of the miraculous or else admitting that the concept of a 'God who acts' has no proper content. The challenge is a healthy one but at least as Dilley puts it it seems to be posed in too stark a form. In the course of the article he quotes a part of the passage from Bultmann which I have already cited and comments: 'Unfor- tunately it does not take much reflection to perceive that although this theory may be very attractive, it is impossible to make it really work.'[4] That Bultmann's conception is a difficult one, that ultimately we may have to admit that it does not really work, I do not want to deny. But I think it does require rather more reflection than Dilley claims. He does not seem to me to pay sufficient attention in his criticisms to the logical oddity of religious language. Has the concept of a 'God who creates man in his own image' no proper content if a wholly evolutionary account of man's origin is accepted? Most of us would say that the evolutionary account is in no way incompatible with the concept of a creator God, whose creating is not identical with but analogous to human creating. It does not seem to me to be any more impossible in principle to speak of an active God whose action is to be seen 'in' rather than 'between' worldly occurrences. Of course the possibility of saying something does not prove its truth. In both cases, creation and divine action in history, it is not enough to argue that the concept is a possible one; we must go on and give grounds to show that it is reasonable to make the particular affirmations concerned.

In the case of creation it is man's experiencing of the world as contingent, as in some fundamental sense given, as not self-explanatory, which has given rise – in my judgment rightly given rise – to the affirmation of God as creator. What then are the grounds which have led men to speak of a God who acts in history? I want to suggest that the conviction is very largely rooted in the fact that so much of the most profound personal experience has about it a quality of response; men have found a meaning and a sense of purpose, bigger than their own comparatively narrow concerns, being elicited as it were by the events of history – sometimes events of an obviously impressive kind, sometimes events of an outwardly insignificant character. What I am trying to describe is not a matter of conscious inference, not a worked out way of explaining experiences to oneself; rather, to use a phrase that John Hick has made familiar in relation to the natural world, it is a matter of 'experiencing-as', of experiencing what happens to us and what we achieve as being in response to an overall purpose at work in the world. It is in the attempt to articulate this way of experiencing life that men have spoken of God as acting in history – a phrase vividly expressing the experience of receptivity which it is intended to express but which can also be dangerously misleading if taken too literally. There is no question of course of this being a kind of deductive proof any more than the cosmological argument can properly be regarded as such; it needs to be seen as one part of that total response to the world in which theism is grounded. All I want to claim here is that there is a fundamental aspect of human experiencing which can suggest a possible line of justification for the kind of talk about divine action which I am trying to explore.

But I have still to face my third question. Even if such a view of divine action is both possible and reasonable, does it do justice to the main traditional affirmations of the Christian faith? This question can be spelt out in a number of different ways. I intend to break it up into two separate questions: (i) can it account for the particularity of the divine action of which Christianity speaks? (ii) is its description of divine-human relationships true to the personal character of God in his dealings with men, as Christian faith understands them, or, to put essentially the same point in a slightly different form, is its account of divine action one in which the word 'action' is being given a proper sense and is something more than a piece of linguistic legerdemain?

(i) First then, the problem of particularity which is so prominent in any Christian account of God's activity in history. I begin once again with a parallel with the doctrine of creation. The natural world, like human history, is an ambiguous mixture of natural evils and natural beauty. Even if we rightly reject any form of Gnostic dualism which seeks to free God from all responsibility for the former, we seem bound to speak of some aspects of the natural world as giving rise more directly to the apprehension of God's creative role than others. I do not think that we can properly speak of God being more creative in one place than in another; the transcendent creator-creature relationship does not permit of being graded in terms of less and more. Nevertheless I think we may speak of certain aspects of the created order as particularly potent vehicles for human awareness of divine creativity.

With this analogy in mind let us turn to the far more acute problem of particularity in historical experience. Not all events elicit equally the sense of response to purposive activity of which I have been speaking. For the Christian the life of Christ, and certain other events also within what is commonly referred to as 'salvation history', have an outstanding potency of this kind and are seen as special divine actions. No one stresses the particularity of the divine action in Jesus Christ more than Bultmann. Since I have used him as my exemplar of a conception of divine action which is sure to appear to some to be seriously 'reductionist' in character, I must in fairness emphasize that he cannot possibly be accused of being 'reductionist' in any sense with regard to the specialness of the divine action in Christ. For him authentic existence (or, in my language, a sense of life as purposive in response to the prior purposive activity of God towards man) can only be realized on the basis of the particular historical event of Jesus Christ. I can only align myself with those who have criticized Bultmann for the absolute and exclusive nature of the claim that he makes here. As Schubert Ogden puts it:

> The New Testament claim 'only in Jesus Christ' must be interpreted to mean not that God acts to redeem only in the event of Jesus and in no other event, but that the only God who acts to redeem any event – *although in fact he redeems every event* – is the God whose redemptive action is decisively revealed in the word which Jesus speaks and is.[5]

But this, of course, does not remove, it only restates, our problem. How can God's action be 'decisively revealed' in certain events and not in others? Can we give any proper meaning to this less exclusive form of affirmation about the special nature of God's action in Christ without falling back into all the difficulties of an action of God which is different in kind from his activity elsewhere, an action which is to be seen 'between' rather than 'in' the worldly occurrences concerned? If we cannot, then whatever the possibility and the reasonableness of conceiving divine action in the way that I am suggesting, we would have to admit that it failed to do justice to the basic affirmations of a distinctively Christian faith. I want to argue – though tentatively and in a way that certainly admits that there may be counter-arguments which will cause me to change my mind – that it is possible, that my proposed conception of divine action is *not* incompatible with speaking of God's redemptive action as 'decisively revealed in the word which Jesus speaks and is'.

I have claimed that it is in the experiencing of life as having the quality of response that the reality of divine action is known. This is in line with Bultmann's oft-repeated warnings against a false objectification of God. It does not mean that the whole concept of God or of divine action is purely subjective in the pejorative sense of that elusive term, which would imply that they were simply ways of describing certain human feelings. It does mean however that the idea of divine action cannot be extracted from its context of being experienced and then considered in isolation from all forms of human response. In some words of Daniel Williams: 'Every "act of God" is presented to us in, through and with the complex of nature and life in which we are. When we say God elected Israel or that he sends his rain on the just and the unjust, we must not ignore the complex analysis of assignable causes and factors in Israel's history or in the cosmic record of rainfall. We have no way of extricating the acts of God from their involvement in the activities of the world.'[6]

Now it is an inevitable feature of the variety to be found within human history that some people by virtue of their personality and of their situation are more fully responsive to the divine action than others. Their words and actions in turn will provide a particularly important focus for calling out such responses from others who follow them. And since that quality of life in them to which those others will respond was itself grounded in responsiveness to the divine action, we may rightly speak of the events of their lives as acts of God in a special sense towards those of us who are influenced by them. In calling them special acts of God we would not be implying that there was any fundamental difference in the relation of the divine action to the particular worldly occurrences of their situation; we would be referring to the depth of response and the creative potential for eliciting further response from others embodied in those particular lives or those particular events.

It would be a natural, but I believe ultimately mistaken, fear to imagine that by describing divine action in this way we are giving a purely humanistic account in which the reality of the divine is ultimately obliterated. Rather what we are doing is avoiding the error of thinking that we can ever describe divine action in any other context than that of its experienced response. This approach finds clear and direct expression in some words from Peter Baelz's book, *Prayer and Providence*, where he discusses the problem of how we can speak of more and less in the activity of God. He writes:

God's providential activity is to be discerned in the way in which he meets and overcomes that which stands out against and resists his creative will. Here we see more of him than in any other situation. His activity meets with the creaturely response which it seeks and towards which it is directed. It is fulfilled in the response which it evokes. It penetrates and enables the relatively independent activity of the creature. It supernaturalizes the natural. In such providential and redemptive activity we come to discern a deeper aspect of God's being. There is a 'more' of God to be apprehended here than elsewhere. His word speaks more clearly, his work is more complete. Christians claim to discern such distinctive activity of God in the life and work of Jesus. Thus on the cross, as he makes his final, life-giving act of self-surrender to his Father, Jesus exclaims, 'It is finished', and Christians ascribe in response to this a completion and finality to the divine work. Creator and creature are here at one. The divine love has conquered. God remains eternally the same God; but in and through the obedient response of Jesus his activity is more fully discerned, because more fully expressed. And since it is more fully expressed, there is a very proper sense in which we may speak of God's *special* activity.[7]

Clearly there is both room and need for continuing discussion how far this approach which I have tried to exemplify from that rather lengthy quotation from Peter Baelz can provide an adequate understanding of the saving events of Christian history. For the moment I want simply to claim that it is not in principle incapable of doing justice to the idea of certain events being divine acts of a specially decisive kind – and, as I am suggesting all along, if it is capable of doing so at all it may be expected to do the job in a way which will be free of many of the difficulties that are attendant on more traditional statements of the unique character of certain events in Christian history.

(ii) I must turn to the second charge which might be brought against the approach I **am** advocating, the charge that it cannot do justice to a properly Christian conception of God's action because it does not conceive that activity in a sufficiently personal way. The charge might reasonably be developed along some such lines as these. You, it might be said, have drawn analogies at various points between the view of God's relation to the natural world and that of his relation to history. But, it might be claimed, Christians have been able to accept an account of God's creative relationship to the world which is of a general rather than a varying kind without imperilling the sense of a fully personal religion just because that more variable and personal approach of God to man is to be found in his activity within history. To argue therefore from an analogy with God's creative relationship will not do. That relationship by itself is not adequately personal to sustain the needs and convictions of the religious life. If God's relationship to men were all of the more generalized kind which is implied in our understanding of him as creator, the religious realities to which Christian faith testifies would evaporate. The kind of understanding of God as creator to which we are being led in this modern age is tolerable precisely because it is *not* the measure of all his relationships towards us.

My primary answer to objections of this kind would be that they seem to me to operate with too simplified a conception of God as personal being. The traditional distinction between an I-thou and an I-it relationship has many values in theology but

if applied in too straightforward a manner to divine-human relationships it can lead to an excessively anthropomorphic picture.
God's relationship to man must never be understood in sub-
personal terms but the test of where this is happening is more
reliably to be found in what the relationship as conceived implies
for human life than in what picture of God appears to be involved. We cannot, I have argued, speak significantly of God
or of his acting in an objectified way, wholly separated from the
human response, and it is therefore the total relationship which
must be assessed in determining whether our understanding is true
to a properly personal conception of God. Now the position
which I am tentatively advocating is one in which divine action
is throughout most closely correlated with human responsiveness.
Thus the total relationship, it would seem to me, is being understood in a personal way in every sense in which that can properly
be applied to a theological discussion of divine-human relationships.

But the objection may also be met along somewhat different
lines. I suggested as an alternative formulation of the objection
that it might be questioned whether the kind of divine action
envisaged could properly be regarded as action in any real sense.
This way of putting the problem draws attention to a difficulty
which is attendant upon any attempt to bring together the convictions of biblical religion and a wholehearted insistence on
divine transcendence. It is a recurrent theme at the heart of the
issues with which the Fathers wrestled in the course of that
confluence of Greek philosophy and biblical faith which marks
the first centuries of the Christian era. The classical solutions to
that problem, as seen for example in the writings of Aquinas,
have always had to qualify the notion of divine action in a somewhat embarrassed and equivocating manner. Since God is complete in himself, eternal and changeless being, any talk of his
acting in the world at all – let alone in the specific and particular
ways of which the Christian tradition speaks – must be very
carefully qualified. In Aquinas' own language, 'being related
to God is a reality in creatures but being related to creatures is not

reality in God'.[8] Now of course behind all such language lies
an extremely subtle and complex philosophical position. Nevertheless I think the point still stands that within the main Christian tradition the 'reality' of God's acting has had to be severely
qualified. Schubert Ogden, whose work I have already quoted,
speaks of 'the timeless Absolute of classical metaphysics, who
may be said to act only in some Pickwickian sense that bears no
real analogy to anything we know as action'.[9] He goes on in the
same essay, which is entitled 'What sense does it make to say
"God acts in history"', to make use of the insights of process
philosophy, as outlined by Whitehead and Hartshorne, to
develop a conception of divine action similar to that which I am
advocating here. Dilley ends his article of challenge to the biblical
theologian by looking in the same direction. Its last words are:
'Perhaps someone with one eye on Whitehead and the other on
the Bible will bring in the next era in theology.' Ogden's claim
is that by working along these lines he is enabled to put forward
a view in which the divine actions can be seen as acts of God
in a much more real, though of course still analogical, sense than
when seen in terms of the classical metaphysical tradition. His
account has certainly its own difficulties which I cannot investigate now. But I think he has at least made out a strong case on
the basis of which it is not unreasonable to claim that the account
of divine action which I have been adumbrating not only gives
a sufficiently 'real' sense to the notion of God acting but one that
may even have positive advantages on that score over more
traditional accounts.

I must come back now and try to relate the conception of
divine action which I have been sketching to the notion of
religious authority, and in particular to the authority of the Bible.
Unless we give some kind of special place to the Bible, I do not
see how there could be a distinctively Christian theology at all.
If therefore the existence of the Bible as an authority or its essential contents should prove to be incompatible with the account
that I have given, the argument which I have been trying to
develop would fall apart. The question must therefore be put:

does the Bible as a religious authority conflict with what I have been saying in either the formal or the substantial way which I distinguished at the beginning?

The former need not, I think, detain us very long. In effect I have already answered it in my attempt to show that my view is compatible with speaking of God's redemptive activity as 'decisively revealed in the word which Jesus speaks and is'. If certain events can be given such special importance without implying a different kind of activity on God's part in relation to the worldly occurrences concerned, then clearly the records which partly record and partly constitute such events can properly be regarded as having religious authority without that fact implying any special interventionist activity as responsible either for their composition or for their recognition as authoritative.

Such an approach also opens the way to ascribing some measure of religious authority to the Scriptures of other faiths without necessarily destroying the idea of something distinctive or decisive about the Christian Scriptures in doing so. In the present situation in which Christian theology has to learn to do its task in a way which takes seriously other expressions of religion in the world, this seems to me to be a positive advantage. Just as the Christian understanding of God contains within itself the seeds of criticism which have led to the modification or abandonment of, for example, certain ideas of hell, despite the formal attestation of those ideas within the Christian tradition itself, so I believe the same understanding of God is ultimately incompatible with certain exclusivist conceptions of religious authority despite their substantial presence within the historical tradition of the faith. Modifications of the idea of religious authority along these lines are not simply something that is imposed from without; they arise also from within.

But the second issue – the issue of the compatibility of the biblical contents – is more difficult. In so far as those contents are defined as giving special attention to particular events no new difficulty arises, which I have not already discussed. But the Bible does more than that. It does not merely witness to events, it interprets them; it understands them in a particular way and that way is undoubtedly very different from the way in which I am proposing that they should be understood. There are exceptions but I would judge that almost overwhelmingly the Bible's way of understanding those special events to which it bears witness is one in which the activity of God in relation to the worldly occurrences concerned is conceived to be of a different kind from that which is operative in the general run of worldly occurrences. Is it consistent then to regard the Bible as a religious authority, which as I have said seems to be an inescapable necessity for a Christian theology, and at the same time to transform as drastically as my account would involve its own understanding of those events to which it bears witness?

This issue came to the fore in an extreme form in the recent 'Death of God' controversy. William Hamilton asks the question: 'if Jesus' demonology, cosmology and eschatology (are) taken as first century views, appropriate then, not so now, needing reinterpretation and understanding, but not literal assent, what is inherently different about Jesus' theology?'[10] In other words, once we cease to take over and accept for ourselves the biblical understanding of the world in its totality (if indeed there is or ever was such a thing) by what criterion do we decide what it is proper to accept and what to reject? The question is a fair one, and can be met in two ways. In the first place we may ask whether Jesus' belief in God is not more central to what he stands for than his belief in eschatology and demons, so that if that goes Jesus' person and teaching simply cease to be really interesting. I think a distinction of that kind can be drawn, though it would be grossly misleading to suggest that either the eschatology or demonology were so peripheral that no serious issue at all arose in their case. But secondly and more significantly we need to ask whether there may not be other supporting grounds, in the field of natural theology for example, for continuing to affirm the theology of Jesus in a way which it might not be reasonable to do in the cases of eschatology and demonology.

In trying to apply these two tests to our present case, I would claim that it is the specialness of the events rather than the special way in which the divine action was understood to be operative in them that is most fundamental. I admit that this is not an easy distinction to make but I think that it can be made. And secondly I would claim on the basis of my earlier discussion to have shown (admittedly in very bare outline) that there may be good reason in our total understanding of the world today for continuing to affirm the former and not continuing to affirm the latter. Thus, while I have no desire to disguise or to minimize in any way the extent of the difference between the way that I am proposing for understanding the special divine activity of which the Bible speaks and the Bible's own understanding of it, I do want to argue that this very considerable difference does not prevent me from continuing to regard the Bible as a religious authority of the utmost importance.

'Begin at the beginning, and go on until you come to the end: and then stop.' But the end-point is as hard to identify as the beginning. In stopping at this point, I do not wish to suggest for a moment that I believe myself to have solved the problems which I have been discussing. My hope is rather that I have said enough to provide a sufficiently coherent account of a possible approach to these puzzling questions for others to develop or, more probably, to expose the flaws and shortcomings in what has been said.

12

Looking into the Sun

*An inaugural lecture as Professor of Christian Doctrine
in the University of London*

When Professor Dunstan delivered his inaugural lecture as Frederick Denison Maurice Professor of Moral and Social Theology last term, he did so under the title of 'A Digger Still'; in it he compared the nature of the theological task incumbent upon the holder of that office to the work of a man whose attention is firmly upon the hard soil of contemporary fact: it was there that his eyes were to be fixed in order to find the proper material for his theological study. In giving to this lecture the title 'Looking into the Sun', it is not my intention to suggest that his colleague, the Professor of Christian Doctrine, is to supplement his studies by following a totally different method; it is not my intention to imply that the appropriate posture for a Professor of Doctrine is one in which he uses his spade to lean upon – should he indeed sully his hands at all with so earthy an implement – so that he may seek the material for his theological study in the heavens above him.

The use of the image 'looking into the sun' with reference to religious or theological endeavour has a long history. A story from the early years of the Christian era tells of the visit of an emperor to a certain rabbi, Joshua ben Hananiah, 'I should like to see thy God', said the emperor. 'Indeed,' replied the rabbi, 'that is impossible.' 'But I *will* see him', insisted the emperor. The rabbi led him out into the sunshine during the summer solstice and said, 'Now look at that.' 'I cannot', was the reply. 'The sun', concluded the rabbi, 'is only one of God's servants; and you ought to admit that as you cannot look into it, much less can you behold his glory.'[1] A second example of its use is both nearer to our own time and more directly related to an occasion of this kind. On 26 March 1922, the young Karl Barth, who had moved the previous October from a Swiss pastorate to a professorship at Göttingen, wrote to his friend, Eduard Thurneysen, as follows:

During the term when I keep talking I am able to preserve the sweet illusion that I indeed know something. . . . To make you acquainted with my spiritual condition I will report to you what Berthold von Regensberg (A.D. 1272) once said: 'A man who looks directly into the sun, into the burning radiance, will so injure his eyes that he will see it no more. It is like this also with faith; whoever looks too directly into the holy Christian faith will be astonished and deeply disturbed with his thoughts.'

In other words [Barth continues] this day and night preoccupation with the 'deepest things' without interruptions from thick-headed candidates for confirmation, church caretakers, and such like is often likely to drive one out of his senses. . . . Often it seems to me problematic to what extent it is both good and possible to spend the thirty-four years that still separate me from my retirement at that task 'being deeply disturbed with thoughts'. To be a proper professor of theology one must be a sturdy, tough, insensitive lump, who notices absolutely nothing. . . . Either one day explode or become quite certainly a blockhead? If you can see any third possibility, tell me of it for my comfort.[2]

From these two quotations it would seem, then, that the theologian who interprets his office, in accordance with the etymology of the word, as one in which he is required to practise ordered and reasoned discourse about God may well find that his task may prove to be impossible – and not only thereby futile, but injurious as well.

Differing aspects of theology have appeared at different times to be particularly dangerous and disturbing forms of looking into the sun. A hundred years ago critical study of the Bible in any form was generally regarded in this light.

Whether [writes Stephen Neill in his history of New Testament interpretation] it was Mr. Newman or Dr. Pusey, Lord Shaftesbury or Dean Close, Mr. Gladstone or Dr. Dale, there was very little between them; all accorded the Bible an unqualified reverence, and all believed that, if its inerrancy were successfully impugned, the whole Christian faith would collapse.³

Colenso's treatment of the Pentateuch merited in Liddon's eyes his classification as one of the 'men who are labouring to destroy and blot out the faith of Jesus Christ from the hearts of the English people'.⁴ It may appear surprising today that looking into Pentateuchal sources should have appeared to be a danger-ous form of looking into the sun, but I don't think that it requires any very great exercise of the historical imagination to recognize, not only that it was so, but how easily and naturally it could have been so. That similar critical study of the gospel records should have been regarded in this way is still less matter for surprise; was it not natural to fear with Bishop Stubbs that it was a first step towards 'the day when the Church shall cry out to Jesus of Nazareth "Thou hast deceived me and I was deceived" '?⁵ Yet critical study of the gospels is something which the church for the most part (whether rightly or wrongly) has come to accept as an activity which can be carried on without undue damage to the eyes, an activity which gives rise, no doubt, to many puzzling and perturbing thoughts but not necessarily to those deeply disturbing thoughts that arise from too direct a gaze into the holy Christian faith. Doubtless many factors have contributed towards enabling the church to come to terms with a thoroughgoing critical treatment of the Scriptures. But in my judgment the most important single factor has been the existence of a basic outline of doctrine, related, of course, to the Scriptures but existing now in its own right in practical independence of them. In the faith of Nicaea and of Chalcedon, belief in God the Father, the incarnation and saving work of the Son, the reality of the Holy Spirit's presence in church and sacrament and Christian believer, the substance of the church's faith seemed able to dwell secure and unscathed, whatever the scholars might discover in the course of their critical investigations of the Bible. But to bring to that framework of Christian belief the same rigorous spirit of critical assessment, that would indeed be to look very directly into the sun with all its attendant dangers and difficulties. Yet what other proper task could there be for a Professor of Christian doctrine in an open, secular university?

I did not begin this lecture with the kind of reference to my predecessor in this chair and to his work which is normally commanded by convention on such occasions. To do so might have appeared as doing no more than I was commanded to do, and that would have been the act not only of an unprofitable servant, but of an ungrateful friend. Moreover, the personal contribution which George Woods made to the concept of the study of doctrine with which this lecture is concerned means that he belongs by right to its heart and not simply to its introduction. It was my great good fortune to enjoy the friendship of George Woods for a period of about twenty years; and I can still recall with the utmost vividness, as I know others in my audience can, the deep sense of personal loss with which I first heard the totally unexpected news of his death nearly two years ago. In my judgment he was above all a great teacher, a teacher not only of undergraduates and of postgraduate students, but a continuing teacher of his colleagues. He had a remarkable ability to worm his way into the heart of a problem. He would set about clarifying the concepts in terms of which the problem was normally posed with a meticulous care that seemed at times as if it were about to lapse into a purposeless pedantry, had it not been lightened by so many delightful shafts of humour in the process and had it not so often led, in the end of the day, to new and creative insights of a fundamental kind, which those of us who lacked his percipience and his persistence would never have achieved without his aid. When he came to London in 1964 he deliberately shifted the main centre of his theological concern from questions of philosophy and ethics to the closely related questions of the study of doctrine. To that issue he brought the mature wisdom of many years' experience and his characteristic determination to clarify for himself the fundamental issues of the problem. In the end he had less than two years to give to that task. But within that short time he had not only outlined a way of approach to the teaching of the subject but had also helped to give it concrete form in a wholly new syllabus for the BD doc⸌ trine course which will be taught here for the first time next year. In addition he has also left to us a short paper published posthumously, entitled 'Doctrinal Criticism', setting out the fundamental nature of the discipline required.[6]

The main thesis of that paper can be indicated by quotation of its opening and its closing words. It begins:

Doctrinal criticism is the critical study of the truth and adequacy of doctrinal statements.

It ends:

It [that is, doctrinal criticism] has its dangers to the Christian faith but I believe that, as in the nineteenth century the threat of biblical criticism was met by accepting its proper use, we ought in this century to meet the challenge of doctrinal criticism by a critical acceptance of its possibilities and legitimacy. There can be no true defence of the faith which is not ultimately the same as the defence of the truth.

Between those two statements lies an account of some of the methods by which such a study would have to be pursued: examination of the relation of any doctrinal statement to its historical situation; the analysis of any doctrinal statement into its component parts; investigation of the varying uses of analogy in the various terms employed in any doctrinal statement; dis⸌ tinction of the differing types of proof to which appeal is made; recognition of the variety of ways in which doctrinal statements are combined into systematic wholes; consideration of what point has been selected as the fundamental starting⸌point of a doctrinal system and for what reason.

I have taken that summary of contents from the pencilled notes which I myself made from a typescript copy of the article sent to me by George Woods only about a month before his death. In the accompanying letter he spoke of it as a 'gloomy article' on the duties of a doctrinal critic, and the prospect as a 'daunting' one. The 'gloom' would, I am sure, not have survived long in any personal discussion of its contents, which, alas, was denied me;

the 'daunting' nature of the prospect certainly continues. Indeed, it is increased now that, as one of his former pupils Brian Hebblethwaite has written in *Theology* for September 1967, 'the project's best defence is sadly denied us, namely the patient work of Professor Woods himself in carrying out the task of doctrinal criticism'.

In that article Hebblethwaite argues that the task is indeed more daunting even than George Woods's account might lead one to believe. For while George Woods discusses the objections that fundamentalism and positivism might raise against the whole enterprise of doctrinal criticism, he does not raise the kind of difficulty that emerges from the insights of psychology. Certainly there are those who would claim that religious and doctrinal statements are so powerfully influenced by our desires and our needs, our hopes and our fears, that they are not amenable to the kind of objective and impartial assessment which a discipline of doctrinal criticism would seek to apply. The difficulty is undoubtedly a real one. The psychology of religious belief is a perplexing study, still, comparatively speaking, in its infancy, but likely perhaps before long to take the centre of the stage as a branch of theological study involving a particularly direct and dangerous form of looking into the sun. Nevertheless it does not, I believe, warrant any premature abandonment of the enterprise of doctrinal criticism as something doomed to certain failure in advance.

Just as, in its extreme form, the verification principle tended to reduce to meaninglessness not only theological discourse but, for example, ethics and aesthetics as well, so in any extreme form the psychological argument from man's capacity for self-deception would be likely to undermine the possibility not only of critical theological reasoning but of similar reasoning also in many other spheres of deeply personal experience. In any branch of the *Geisteswissenschaften*, any form of humane study, the task of determining 'what is the case' (to use a favourite and characteristic expression of George Woods) is an enormously complex business. We cannot isolate or eliminate the element of personal interpretation; yet we do not allow that fact to lead us to deny the possibility of sustained critical reasoning in the spheres of litera-ture or drama, of art or ethics. Nor should we do so in the case of doctrine, though we will be well advised to take good note of the very real dangers of self-deception in this field.

There are certain academic disciplines in which it is easier to do the job itself than to describe to one's own satisfaction (let alone the enlightenment of others) the method by which one is attempting to proceed; there are others in which it is easier to describe than to do. Doctrinal criticism seems to me to fall into the latter category. A single inaugural lecture provides ample excuse for staying wholly and safely within the realm of descrip-tion of method. Nevertheless I want to attempt in the second half of this lecture to give some idea of how this understanding of the task of doctrinal study might work in actual practice. To do so, I propose to sketch – obviously in the very barest outline – the way in which the doctrinal critic might approach one of the central tenets of Christian doctrine; and I have chosen for that purpose the church's conviction about the uniqueness or finality of Christ, the ἐφ' ἅπαξ, the *Einmaligkeit*, the once-for-allness, of Christ and of his work which has been from the beginning a prominent feature of Christian belief and of Christian teaching. Uniqueness, of course, can be used in varying senses. There is a weak sense in which each individual person is unique. But when Christians have spoken of the uniqueness of Christ they have certainly meant more than that. The more that they have meant is often described by saying that he is different from all others not only in degree, but in kind. Whether that way of stating the difference be regarded as a satisfactory one or not, it points clearly enough to the strong sense of uniqueness with which I am con-cerned; and I shall indicate the fact by speaking of Christ's *radical* distinctiveness or uniqueness. Now there are some people who are so firmly rooted in the Christian tradition which has not only nurtured, but been nurtured by, this kind of conviction that they do not find it an intolerably odd or difficult conception. I stress the word 'intolerably', because even within the most central and orthodox Christian tradition the oddity and the difficulty of the conception has certainly been felt.

From the earliest days the problem has always been to pass beyond the purely formal statement of this basic conviction and to succeed in spelling out its implications in convincing terms. The history of Christian doctrine is littered with attempts to understand the person of Christ and his saving work, the attractiveness of which has been strongly felt for a time but which have ultimately been discarded as failing to fulfil this condition of what a properly Christian doctrine needs to affirm. Accounts of the incarnation based on the analogy of our human experience of divine grace from Theodore of Mopsuestia to Donald Baillie, so-called 'subjective' theories of the atonement from Abélard to Hastings Rashdall, have had a strong appeal as providing intellectually intelligible and religiously attractive accounts of Christ and of his work; yet as statements of Christian doctrine they have generally been dubbed inadequate on the one ground of their failure to do justice to the radical distinctness of Christ's person and to the objective character of his work. Thus this fundamental feature of Christian conviction has been strongly maintained, but not without awareness of its problematic character. The doctrinal critic of today is bound in my judgment to feel the oddity and the difficulty of this kind of Christian assertion in a very acute form as he tries to relate Christian doctrine to his contemporary understanding of the world and of human knowledge about the world as a whole.

How, then, is the doctrinal critic to proceed? He begins by examining this conviction within the historical setting in which it first arose. Here he needs to work in very close liaison with those of his colleagues who are specialists in the field of biblical and New Testament studies. When he does so, he is likely to conclude that the strong sense of Christ's absolute uniqueness as expressed in later doctrinal conviction is not something which emerges at all directly from the original teaching of Jesus himself – in so far as we are able to determine the precise content of that teaching with any confidence. Rather it is something which

comes to consciousness within the life of the church which
stemmed from him. Yet even here it does not seem to be the case
that the radical nature of the conviction of the once-for-allness
of Christ's work can be wholly accounted for as a necessary
conclusion to be drawn from the new quality of life expressed
in the early church. However profoundly transforming such an
experience may have been, it could not logically be claimed to
require as its cause a person or a happening of the radically
unique kind which Christian doctrine has always affirmed.
That would be to commit the same kind of fallacy as is generally
agreed to be involved in any direct argument from the contingent
and limited world to an absolute and infinite God. Rather we
must say that the initial sense of the finality of Jesus and his work
was due to the interpretation of those experiences to which his
mission gave rise within an already existing framework of
eschatological belief. If your overall view of the world and of
God's dealing with the world is one which looks for some
literally final cataclysmic event which will bring the whole
process to its destined goal, then the work (if not necessarily the
person) of the one who brings in that ultimate event must
logically be seen as distinct in kind from the work of all his
predecessors, who by definition were only part of an ongoing
process and not the final term in the series.

It was within this eschatological context – the context alike of
Jesus' own mission and of his first followers' proclamation of
him immediately after his death and resurrection – that a sense
of the radical ultimacy of Christ's work first took place. But
that context did not remain static. It underwent at the very least
two important changes in the immediately ensuing centuries. In
the first place the literal completion of the course of history –
originally an integral part of the eschatological context of belief –
did not take place either at the culmination of Jesus' ministry or
in its immediate aftermath. With this fact the church had to
come to terms – and did so. The ultimacy of Christ's work might
at the first have been understood literally and chronologically;
but, it came to be felt, it did not need to be so understood. One

day to God is as a thousand years; the ultimacy of Christ's work
could still be affirmed, even though it were not literally the
ultimate event of world history. But a second, even greater,
transposition took place with the move of the church's centre of
gravity from a Semitic to a Greek setting. In this case not only
the temporal immediacy but the whole eschatological view
proved ill at ease. The religious aspirations of the Greek world
were couched not in terms of an expected fulfilment of the
historical process but rather in terms of a changeless divine realm,
whose divine quality consisted, in part at least, in the fact of its
complete separation from that historical process. In that setting
the church's understanding of Christ and of his work came to
be expressed primarily in terms of divine and human natures and
of the effective inculcation of immortal, divine life into mortal,
finite substance. It was not easy in such terms to give expression
to the sense of the ultimacy of Christ's role, but with struggle the
task was achieved; it was achieved by affirming that in Christ
was to be found a conjunction of the two natures in one person
through the utterly unique – to use the technical term, the hypostatic – union of God and man in the incarnation. In that form,
it has been handed on to all subsequent generations in the famous definition of Chalcedon.

We live in an age for which the later Platonism of the fourth
century AD is almost – almost, but not quite – as alien an outlook
as the eschatological expectations of late Judaism. We too, therefore, are continuously involved in an activity of attempted
transposition of doctrinal affirmations. One of the main features
of the general outlook of our age can be indicated by the designation 'historical relativism'. I am not suggesting that by this I
mean some clear-cut and precise set of convictions before which
modern man must bow uncritically as before some unchallengeable idol. By it I want to refer (since this is obviously not the
place for any extended critical discussion) simply to the way in
which we all see things today in terms of their place in the course
of historical development; I intend simply a reminder of the way
in which when we think and speak most carefully we recognize

the need to assess particular occurrences in relation to the particular limited circumstances of their time and place – and indeed to allow that our own assessments must be assessed in that way. From such a standpoint it is not difficult to give varying degrees of importance to differing historical events; but it is very difficult to give to any historical events, however superlative their degree of importance, the kind of radical ultimacy that Christianity appears to ascribe to the life, death, and resurrection of Jesus.

Now the traditional way for the doctrinal student to deal with this problem is to take the unique status of Christ as defined, for example, in the Chalcedonian formula of the one person who is both fully God and fully man, and then to wrestle with contemporary thought about the world at its best until the two can be shown to be compatible notions. This is not sheer obscurantism; it can be done, as it is done for example by the Jesuit scholar Karl Rahner in an essay entitled 'Christology within an evolutionary view of the world', with great sensitivity and great erudition – and, I think one must add, in his case with great obscurity also.[7]

But this way of proceeding is barred to the doctrinal critic. However much weight he may properly attach to certain traditional doctrinal convictions, he cannot allow to *any* a position of absolute privilege, a position from which they cannot be called in question. This is not to say that all doctrinal affirmations must be expected to shrivel up and disappear the moment they are blown upon by the cold breath of an inhospitable age. In the present case it might prove that, if we paid careful enough attention to the totality of our experience, to (for example) the experience of the absoluteness of moral demand, then our sense of historical relativism would come to be modified in a way which provided more scope for affirming the radical uniqueness of the events of the life, death, and resurrection of Jesus. It might be so, but we have also to consider the other possibility that it might not. We might also be led to judge that this sense of the radical uniqueness of Jesus was not a part of the inner substance of Christian faith in the way in which it has generally been conceived, but rather a part of the historically relative form in which response to his life, death, and resurrection was first articulated. I believe there are certain pointers to suggest that this might well turn out to be the case.

One of the most important contributions to christology in very recent years is the work of Wolfhart Pannenberg, Professor of Systematic Theology at Mainz. In his work *Grundzüge der Christologie*, he claims that christology must be established on the basis of the history of Jesus critically studied. He believes that it is possible to establish on that basis the reality of the resurrection as worthy of belief on historical grounds. (That, I need hardly add, is a highly disputable and much disputed statement, but the dispute is irrelevant to the point I want to make here.) For, however that may be, the resurrection by itself, is not, in Pannenberg's view, a sufficient ground on which to base the confession of Jesus' divinity. The important fact, he insists, is that Jesus proclaimed the imminence of the apocalyptic end (which would have included universal resurrection) in connection with his own person and his own mission. But the end did not come; what did come was the resurrection of Jesus alone. Within the context of the apocalyptic hope this resurrection of Jesus came to be understood as an anticipation of the general resurrection and thereby an anticipation of the end of history. That understanding of it and that understanding of it alone justifies the ascribing of an absoluteness of revelation to the person and work of Jesus, because absoluteness of revelation can only come at the end of history; absoluteness of revelation, Pannenberg argues, could not occur within the relativity of an ongoing, uncompleted historical process. Absoluteness of revelation is logically incompatible with being part of a necessarily relative process. 'Why the man Jesus can be the ultimate revelation of God,' he writes, 'why in him and only in him God is supposed to have appeared, remains incomprehensible apart from the horizon of the apocalyptic expectation.'[8] For Pannenberg, therefore, the grounds for ascribing ultimacy and full divinity to Christ are logically tied to interpreting him in an apocalyptic context. Not surprisingly this issue has been taken up and challenged in reviews of his work. A quotation from one review which has been repeated with approval in subsequent discussion poses the matter thus: 'The main question the reviewer should ask is this: What compels us to accept "the horizon of the apocalyptic expectation" of later Judaism in order to perceive God's revelation in Jesus?'[9] But may it not be that there is a measure of truth both in Pannenberg's contention and in the challenge of his critics? Pannenberg may well be right in suggesting that the *radical* ultimacy of Christ's work and the *full* divinity of his person can be affirmed meaningfully only within the context of apocalyptic expectation; within a context, that is to say, which expects the immediate and dramatic culmination of all history. But his critics may also be justified in questioning whether such a context is essential for there to be *any* perception of God's revelation in Jesus. If there is validity in both positions, and if, as Pannenberg's reviewers imply and most of us I think would agree, we cannot in fact live today within such a context, this would not mean that we had to abandon all perception whatsoever of God's revelation in Jesus but it would mean that we might have to abandon our expression of that revelation in any of the traditional forms of substantial divinity and of ultimate, objective saving work.

May I emphasize that I put that forward as the kind of conclusion to which the doctrinal critic might be led by seeking first to examine critically a fundamental doctrinal conviction within the historical setting of its origin and then to relate it to his own contemporary understanding of the world. Obviously such arguments require far more thorough examination than I have been able to give them here before their proper force can be evaluated. Indeed, they require far more thorough examination not only than I have been able to give them here in this lecture but than I have as yet been able to give them at all. For I would stress that I have ventured to put before you not finished conclusions but a sketch of the kind of issue and the kind of method with which the work of doctrinal criticism will need, I believe, to concern itself in the future. I do not hesitate to confess that the process does give rise, for myself, as I suspect it will for others, to deeply disturbing thoughts. But unless the method can be shown to be false it must be pursued. 'There can be no true defence of the faith which is not ultimately the same as the defence of the truth.' We do well to remember that in the past the church has had to revise her beliefs about, for example, the expected immediacy of the end and the inerrancy of the biblical account of the words of Jesus, without finding herself as a result forced to act as Bishop Stubbs so greatly feared and to reproach her master with the words 'Thou hast deceived me and I was deceived'.

It is important to be clear what would and what would not be implied were a doctrinal critic to be led to the kind of judg⁄ment which I have very tentatively put forward. He would not be saying: 'I might have ascribed to Jesus substantial divine status and to his death an objective effect altering the status of men as sinners but in fact I do not see sufficient grounds for doing so.' Rather he would be saying: 'People have made these kinds of affirmation in the past within the context of a world⁄view which it is no longer possible for me to share. Their affirmations were intimately bound up with that world⁄view of a bygone age. They are therefore for me no longer live options; I am not in a position either to affirm them or to deny them; I cannot give any satisfactory sense to them *in that form*'. At first it might seem that this is an even more damaging criticism than the other. Is it not worse to say of someone that he is talking non⁄sense than to say that he is wrong? But that would be a very superficial and misleading way of putting it. The fact that the doctrinal critic's world⁄view is different and that from his stand⁄point he cannot give satisfactory connotation to the doctrinal statements of the past does not mean that he has to regard those statements as nonsense in the common⁄or⁄garden meaning of that word. At the very least, to borrow language which kindly⁄disposed linguistic philosophers used sometimes to apply to theologians, it would be a highly significant kind of nonsense; but there is no real justification for using the word 'nonsense' at all, however kindly qualified. The doctrinal critic, who is also himself a Christian, is likely to treat it as a working assumption that it is worthwhile worrying away at what lies at the heart of, underneath, or at the back of, traditional doctrinal statements; in their old form they may no longer make satisfactory sense for him in relation to his honest attempts to understand the world in which he lives in all its depth, but that is not the same thing as to say that he regards them as unimportant or valueless. He will press on analysing the language used, studying the different kinds of proof on which men have relied, seeing the different ways in which those beliefs have been fitted into systematic presentations of doctrine. At the same time, he will try to fit together the insights which he gains from this process with those which he gains from a patient, continuing study of the world around him. To speak of 'fitting together' the insights from two such disparate sources is a dangerous way of speaking. It suggests that one at least is liable to be distorted in order to achieve a fit. Every Christian theologian must expect the charge of being unfaithful either to the historical tradition of Christian faith or to the realities of the modern world. But that is no argument against the propriety of the task. In any attempt to describe human experience in a unified way we are bound to be involved in bringing together insights drawn from widely differing perspec-tives. Certainly, if we are to minimize the very real danger of distortion, our appraisal of both the traditional and the con-temporary must be equally careful and equally critical. There will be plenty of digging for the doctrinal critic to do alongside his colleagues in both historical and contemporary studies. Look-ing into the sun implies no exemption from the work of digging.

But it is also possible for a professor of doctrine to evade his responsibilities by too much digging – and that may well prove the greater temptation. His digging will never be completed; yet it must not absorb all his energies. Neither he nor his students are to be allowed to avoid the danger and the difficulties of disturb-ing thoughts by remaining exclusively at the level of historical inquiries. On the basis of those inquiries they have also to look into the heart of their most holy faith and say as best they may what they discern there. Whether, for one who pursues that course over the years, the third possibility for which Karl Barth asked in addition to the 'one day explode or become quite certainly a blockhead' really exists remains to be seen. Radically as my own approach to theology differs from his (if I may be allowed to compare such incomparables), I would certainly want to say that Karl Barth's continued activity as a Christian thinker of undiminished vigour, forty-six years after those words which I have quoted were first written, gives me some hope that that third way must after all exist. And if *not*? – well, I take comfort from the fact that the powers that be in this college have allocated to the Professor of Christian Doctrine a room at the top of the department of War Studies; that fact I interpret as implying that, if there is no third way, if in the end the choice must lie between explosion and blockheadedness, the former is (in their judgment) the more likely eventuality. For that compliment I thank them, as I thank also all those here who have done me the honour of being present on this occasion.

13

Jerusalem, Athens, and Oxford

*An inaugural lecture as Regius Professor of Divinity
in the University of Oxford*

My first teaching post in an English university was to fill a
vacancy in Cambridge created by Dr Chadwick's appointment
as Regius Professor of Divinity in this university. In the September just before I took up that post I met a student whom I knew
slightly and who was half-way through his theological course
at Cambridge. He was kind enough to congratulate me on my
appointment, and then with that combination of honesty and
insensitivity that is so characteristic of the young he added
'though, of course, no one could possibly match Henry Chadwick's superb lectures on early Christian doctrine'. That senti-
ment was one of which I was already sufficiently well aware to
feel that I did not perhaps need so blatant a reminder of it. Now
that I find myself in the same position once again, the same senti-
ment applies once more with equal force. To me the outstanding
feature of Dr Chadwick's scholarship is the way in which he
combines massive and detailed learning with grace and simplicity of style. There are many scholars who are learned and dull,
not a few who are superficial and lively, some who manage to be
superficial and dull – but to be learned and lively to the degree in
which both epithets characterize Dr Chadwick's writing and
lecturing is the achievement of very few.

The field of early Christian doctrine, of which he is so pre-
eminently the master, has many fascinations. For me its particular
fascination is the attempt to understand the ways in which a
gospel of Jewish origin came to find expression in the very
different medium of Graeco-Roman thought. What has Athens

to do with Jerusalem? The question was asked by Tertullian as early as the year 200. And the implied answer is nothing. That question has gone on being asked down the centuries and has received the most diverse answers. Some, like Tertullian, have seen Athens as the distorting mirror which must be got firmly out of the way if the light of the gospel of Jesus is to shine on us in its true colours once more. Others have seen Athens as the essential prism through which we need to look at the brilliant but confused lights of the original kaleidoscopic gospel if we are to see there the true picture and not one of the many counterfeit biblicisms with which the world still abounds today. What these two diametrically opposed approaches to the Fathers have in common is that they both appear to know what the essential Christian truth is. The study of early Christian doctrine is of importance to them both. For the one it helps to reveal what Christian truth is negatively; for the other it reveals what that truth is positively. But a sensitive study of early doctrine will not leave us for long content with either thesis. The truth is more complex than either approach allows.

No ingredient of patristic study is a better dissolvent of all such oversimplified theories than the study of Origen. 'In toto Origene', wrote Luther, 'non est verbum unum de Christo'[1] – not a single word in the whole of Origen about Christ; and with that judgment contrast the words of Charles Bigg: 'The Cross in all its wonder, its bounty, its power is always before the eyes of Origen.'[2] The divergence of judgment is not solely due to the different standpoints of the two interpreters. Part of the fascination of Origen (and finding him the most fascinating of all the Fathers is something which I suspect I share with my predecessor) is that the same person can read Origen and at the same time feel the pull of both judgments. He simply refuses to fit into any of the ready-made pigeon-holes into which we try to place him. Dr Chadwick ends his most attractive book on *Early Christian Thought and the Classical Tradition* in characteristically perceptive and tantalizing fashion. 'We tend', he writes, 'to begin the study of Origen by asking whether or not he is

orthodox, and find that in the process we are continually driven
back to the prior question: what is the essence of orthodoxy?'[3]

None of Dr Chadwick's forerunners in that Oxford patristic
tradition, which he has done so much to enhance and make
known in centres of learning throughout the world, would have
questioned the exactitude of his scholarship; they would have
acclaimed in him someone who knows his texts with the same
kind of intimacy that they themselves had and that they so
strongly advocated. But some of them would, I suspect, have
been rather disturbed by his question. For our predecessors of a
century ago the essence of orthodoxy was not a problematic concept. Patristic scholarship in their view served not to complicate
the issue but to clarify it. They could not, it is true, claim that
the study of the Fathers was self-evidently congruous with Anglican doctrine at every point – for had not 'study of the Fathers'
been, by Newman's own assertion, the very thing that had led
him to Rome? But they could and did believe that patristic
teaching properly understood would coincide in substance
with true Anglican doctrine and would help to clarify it.
Thus in the course of the fierce debate about baptismal regeneration set in motion by the Gorham judgment, J. B. Mozley, who
was appointed Regius Professor of Divinity here exactly 100
years ago, could quote (in his order) Chrysostom and Basil,
Ambrose and Tertullian, Hermas and Clement of Alexandria,
Jerome and Hilary, Gregory Nazianzen and Gregory Nyssen,
Cyprian and Origen, Hippolytus and Cyril of Alexandria,
Justin, Augustine and Theodoret, and go on to argue their
agreement with one another and their authority for us in these
terms.

Language which has two opposite meanings has no meaning, and
language which has no meaning has no authority. In that case [namely,
if there is inconsistency or confusion in what they state] the patristic language on the subject of baptismal regeneration ceases to be a ground on
which any doctrine of any kind on that subject can be raised. And in
forming our judgement on this question, we must put the whole of it
aside, as so much inextricable confusion and useless lumber, clogging the

question instead of clearing it, and intercepting explanation instead of aiding it. But . . . I would claim that this language should be regarded as not having two contradictory meanings, but one meaning – that is to say, as being consistent and rational language. I would insist on that *rationale* of it which is the favourable one to patristic authority, and which all admirers of the Fathers will adopt.[4]

Thus the clarification of patristic teaching and the defence of orthodoxy were felt to go hand in hand.

It was this kind of conviction which caused so much difficulty at the time of the foundation of the Oxford Theological School. To Pusey, who bitterly opposed any such innovation in 1854, it seemed that there was a simple choice: 'The examiners must necessarily be judges of orthodoxy,' he declared, or else 'the new School of Theology will become a School of indifferentism to truth.'[5] Yet it was Pusey who was the prime proponent of the introduction of the Theological School some fourteen years later. Supporters of the new School at that time felt able to insist that 'the examiners, it will be pretty generally admitted by persons not on their legs in debate, will not have it for their primary object to test soundness of opinion'[6] and that every candidate could be assured that 'to certify the world of his *Orthodoxy* will never certainly be the intention of his Examiners.'[7] What then had become of indifferentism to truth? The difficulty was claimed to be unreal because unsound views would be rejected – not because they were unsound, but because they were erroneous. When in the course of the protracted debates before the founding of the School, the Professor of Geometry asked what would happen if a candidate were to 'attribute (in common with seven-tenths of Christendom) the doctrine of Transubstantiation to the Antenicene Church,'[8] he was told that such a candidate would indeed

find it a hard matter to persuade any examiner in his right mind to reward him with a First Class, for his assertion would be almost as silly as if one of your candidates were to deny that the three angles of a triangle are equal to two right angles. . . . These are not matters of opinion but of fact. That the man would suffer, is likely enough; but it would not be for his

Opinions that he would suffer. It would be for his Ignorance. It may be calamitous that the truths of Divinity are not of the same kind as the truths of Mathematics; but it is unavoidable.[9]

It does not sound a very promising start to the new School. The preface to a new edition of Cyril's three epistles prepared explicitly for the use of the new School in 1872 reminds the reader that 'they [including, that is, the notorious third letter with the twelve anathemas] have come down to us . . . with the sanc' tion of (one or more) Oecumenical Councils and are conse' quently, these being the Act of the whole Church, binding on the whole Church.'[10] But general patristic teaching is never treated as beyond the range of critical assessment. Early examina' tion papers for example often invite criticism of Athanasius's exegesis of the Old Testament. Most of the questions indeed in the Dogmatica section are of a straightforwardly historical kind. But there are exceptions in the earliest papers. Thus in 1873 the candidate was instructed to 'establish the Divinity and the Personality of the Holy Ghost' and to write about 'the Doxology of Polycarp and the incorrect argument founded on it'; a ques' tion in 1874 reads: 'He descended into Hell. In what creed were these words first inserted? Have they always been understood in the same sense? What do you understand by them and by what texts do you prove them? Why is it important that we should believe in this article of the Faith?' In 1876 he is asked to 'Maintain the position of the English Church as to the suffi' ciency of the Holy Scriptures for Salvation', and in 1878 to 'Shew, with instances, that the Ante'Nicene Christian writers held Nicene doctrines'. But before long the questions have be' come in practice indistinguishable from those which might face a student today in a paper on the History of Early Doctrine.

Nevertheless the problem of orthodoxy remained a bug'bear. Debate centred around the restriction of examiners for Schools and of candidates for higher degrees to priests in Anglican orders. The fear of those who opposed reform was whether, if the examinations were taken out of the hands of churchmen, the School would remain 'orthodox' and Christian.[11] Those who committed the cardinal sin, of which every late recruit to this university has to beware, of quoting Cambridge precedent were told in an appeal to Convocation that the precedent was irrelevant because Dogmatics did not occupy nearly so prominent a place in the Cambridge examination.[12] But by 1913 the Dean of Christ Church and all the Divinity Professors (including Strong, Lock, and Ottley who had all signed the appeal to Convocation against it nine years earlier) joined together to support the change on the ground that 'the University, constituted as it is, is no longer qualified to give a certificate of orthodoxy.'[13] The opposition was vigorous and vociferous – but one senses a note of desperation in the contorted argument that the opening of higher degrees to all comers might in practice result in compelling an orthodox Regius Professor to recommend a learned heretic for the Doctorate of Divinity and that the evil of such a possibility was in no way mitigated by the unhappy fact (apparently introduced into the debate by Dr Lock) that the system of crown appointments might one day lead to an unorthodox Regius Professor of Divinity himself being foisted upon the university.[14]

Well, perhaps it might; perhaps by now it has. But the signatories of the flysheet may not only have been guessing about an unwelcome future. For Dr Hampden's appointment long before in 1836 had been greeted in just such terms. Mozley objected to Hampden's Bampton lectures mainly on the grounds that Hampden 'uses the words "heterodox" and "orthodox" throughout the lectures with the most perfect impartiality between the two, thinking both equally wrong as being dogmatizers.'[15] The form of Mozley's complaint is interesting, for it clearly reveals the interrelation between the approach to patristic studies on the one hand and to questions of 'orthodoxy' and 'heterodoxy' on the other. For the central thesis of Hampden's Bampton lectures was that the whole patristic tradition was an incursion of theory into religion, which though necessary for that time, was a disastrous heritage if treated as providing the basis of true religion in subsequent ages. 'Orthodoxy,' he wrote, 'was forced to speak the divine truth in the terms of heretical speculation ... the necessity of the case compelled the orthodox ... to employ a phraseology by which, as experience proves, the naked truth of God has been overborne and obscured.' This approach he applied unflinchingly to the Nicene and Athanasian creeds (but not to the Apostles' creed which in his view stated 'nothing but facts' and was in striking contrast to the scholastic speculations involved in the Nicene and Athanasian creeds[16]). Those creeds, he declares, would in their own day have been 'readily interpreted by the existing physical and logical notions', but today apart from previous study of the existing state of theology and philosophy at that time, they 'are as if they were written in a strange language. The words, indeed, are signs of ideas to us, but not of those ideas which were presented to the minds of men, when the formularies were written or when they were adopted by the Church.'[17] Mozley on the other hand gives a very different account of the role of philosophy in relation to the creeds. His appointment as Regius Professor of Divinity coincided with the controversy about the use of the damnatory clauses of the Athanasian creed. In his professorial lectures delivered in the Latin Chapel of Christ Church Cathedral he included a special lecture in defence of their use. (In parenthesis it may be added, a lecture so successful that those clauses are still on occasion to be heard in that chapel – but that is another story.) In the course of it he insists that the creed 'was composed for persons who wanted their ears to ring with the doctrine of the Trinity' but that 'it was the very interest of the Creed, if I may say so, to avoid metaphysics. Speculation was foreign to its aim.'[18]

The difference between them could perhaps be put in this way. For Hampden Jerusalem and Athens had little to do with one another. Their moods were too far apart. That did not mean that he thought the Fathers had got the gospel wrong. He put his position in conciliatory form in his inaugural lecture as Regius Professor of Divinity. It was a tense occasion and in its preparation he lost, we are told, both sleep and appetite, his chief nourishment being what his wife's anxious care would place by his side as he wrote.[19] In the lecture he affirmed that he was satisfied in his own mind that the Creeds and the Articles had been of essential use in maintaining the Christian religion in its integrity and it was from within that conviction that he had said what he had said on occasion in criticism of the abstract phraseology in which they were expressed.[20] In effect his position seems to be that the Fathers had made the best of a bad job. They were orthodox, which was for him an unfortunate yet necessary thing to be, of essentially temporary significance. Hampden's detractors were always rather puzzled and irritated by the fact that he never appeared in practice to be as unorthodox as they felt him to be in essence. And they were not wholly wrong. There was dynamite in his method, but he was not the kind of person actually to ignite it. For Mozley, on the other hand, Jerusalem and Athens stood much closer together. The dogmatic intention of the patristic age had been 'to preserve the original idea, mystery as it was, unaltered, to keep truth as it stood,'[21] and in that aim it had gloriously succeeded. Precisely the same divergence of judgment emerges with regard to the Articles. The XVIIth Article which concerns predestination and election is described by Hampden as a wise authoritative statement of the reformers called forth by the state of opinion at the time and derived 'from their own education in the theories of Scholasticism', the original mode in which the issue at stake had been theoretically propounded.[22] For Mozley, on the other hand, it gives 'a plain unpretending summary of the language of St. Paul'.[23] Now Mozley is generally regarded as having had a far better mind than Hampden – and I find that judgment confirmed by a survey of their writings. Nevertheless I am equally convinced that on this issue Hampden was a great deal nearer to the truth than Mozley.

Historical studies, pursued along the line of Hampden's approach, soon give rise to Dr Chadwick's question: What is the essence of orthodoxy? It is possible to refuse to tackle the question. The Theological School at Oxford could have remained content to let Dogmatica rest at the level of exclusively historical inquiry. The relation between Athens and Jerusalem is, as I have said, a fascinating study in its own right. But if that is where the inquiry stops, its proper place would be in some Sub-Faculty of the History of Ideas. For the theologian the further question is inescapable. Not only: what did they believe and why? but were they right? what is true opinion? what is orthodoxy? Not only: what has Athens to do with Jerusalem? but what has Athens or Jerusalem to do with Oxford?

Even when in 1905 the required paper in the Dogmatic section became (as it still is) 'The history of Christian doctrine to AD 461', a directly doctrinal paper was included in the list of possible special subjects. But in that capacity it was taken only once, in 1909. Since 1921 there have been periods when such a paper was available as an alternative to the early history of doctrine. But it does not seem to have been greatly used. In the thirteen years between the end of the war and 1958 there were more years when no paper was required than when one was; and in 1959 it was returned to the limbo of special subjects, which meant that it was no longer taken at all.

It was only with the introduction of an entirely new paper with a new status, 'The Christian Doctrines of God, Human Nature and Salvation', set for the first time in 1964, that directly doctrinal work really reappears with a substantial position in the life of the Theology School. The suggestion for the new paper was first officially made in a letter to the Chairman of the Faculty of Theology on 28 February 1962. By 8 June of the same year it had received the approval of the Faculty, the Faculty Board, and the General Board. The only significant change in that three-month period is that where the initial letter had spoken of the failure of a faculty 'organized on a mainly historical basis . . . to meet the needs of the Church', the preamble to the General Board Report spoke rather of its failure 'to provide sufficient opportunity for the study of recent theological developments'. When one reflects upon the importance of the principle involved – and also on the average length of time it takes to get anything through any series of boards at the present moment – it was a noteworthy achievement.

It did not, of course, constitute a simple return to the approach which I have tried to illustrate from some of the earliest Schools examination papers. The concept of Christian doctrine involved is clearly a much more open and flexible one. Three questions taken from the 1969 paper illustrate the difference of approach. Candidates were asked:

In what sense, if any, would you deem it right to speak of God as personal?

How far is it (*a*) necessary, (*b*) possible for a Christian to believe both that God is sovereign and that man is free?

To what extent must Christianity retain the idea of the miraculous?

The questions seem designed to leave the candidate free to assert that God should not be spoken of as personal; that either the sovereignty of God or the freedom of man may have to be denied; and that the idea of the miraculous may be at least very nearly dispensable. I can envisage candidates putting forward such theses in a way which would persuade their examiners to reward them with a first class – their examiners being men in their right minds in so far as that is a possible condition for examiners to be in at the end of their allotted task.

Why is it that questions of doctrine arise for us in so much more open and radical a fashion today? It might seem natural to suggest that the main reason is that we live in an age when Christian faith is under challenge of a far more radical and searching kind than in the past. Probably it is. Yet Christians of almost every age have felt themselves faced with unbelief of a much more radical nature than any previous generation. When Mozley was appointed Regius Professor in 1871, Pusey wrote to him in these terms:

My dear Mozley – How strangely different are the times in which you return to us from those in which you left us [namely in 1856 when Mozley had married and taken a college living at Shoreham]. Now the fight is not for fundamentals even, but as to the existence of a personal God, the living of the soul after death, or whether we have any soul at all; whether there is or can be any positive truth except as to physics etc. . . . But we have a great battle; I for whatever time remains to me, you, I hope, during many years of vigour. It is an encouragement that the battle is so desperate. All or nothing; as when the Gospel first broke in upon heathen philosophers; and the fishermen had the victory.[24]

The language of the closing phrases betrays a past age, but the earlier part might well have been written much nearer to our own time. It is not so much in the assessment of the nature of the challenge that we differ, as in the way we feel we have to meet it.

For Hampden was in no greater doubt than Mozley where the truth lay, even if he was far less convinced of the adequacy or the permanence of traditional ways of expressing it. Over against all Creeds and Articles Hampden speaks of an 'immutability . . . which we ascribe properly to Scripture facts alone' and of 'the fundamental doctrines themselves – *the revealed facts* – which are really and in themselves, independent of the theories.'[25] And Mozley declares against those who find Scripture obscure that it 'is indeed but too plain, its truths too express, if we are to judge by the extraordinary difficulty there is in explaining them away'; 'upon the great truths of the Christian Creed I do not think there can be any fair doubt as to what Scripture says.'[26] For them both Jerusalem at least spoke with a clear voice, and what Jerusalem had to say was what had (with comparatively minor modifications of form) to be said in Oxford in their day. On this they were at one, however different their evaluation of the role of Athens on the way. But it is precisely on that point of their agreement with one another that I at least find myself furthest from them. The reasons for so fundamental a change in the approach to religious truth have often been discussed and I do not intend to discuss them in any detail today. Of primary importance has been the impact of a detailed historical study of the biblical writings and the growth of a more general historical consciousness among ourselves. The heart of the matter is put trenchantly by Wolfhart Pannenberg when describing the fundamental difference which a modern Lutheran theologian finds between himself and Luther. 'Luther,' he writes, 'could still identify his own doctrine with the content of the biblical writings, literally understood. For us, on the contrary, it is impossible to overlook the historical distance between every possible theology today and the primitive Christian period. This distance has become the source of our most vexing theological problems.'[27] Jerusalem no less than Athens belongs to its age and not to ours.

What then are we to do with those most vexing theological problems which arise from the historical and cultural distance of both Jerusalem and Athens from Oxford? How is the theologian to proceed? I want to outline the kind of answer that I believe has to be given to that question (and clearly I cannot here do more than give the barest of outlines) by means of some comments on Professor Macquarrie's inaugural lecture on 'Creation and Environment' delivered here last term.[28] In talking about the roots of the Christian doctrine of creation, he very properly warned us, as any sensitive scholar is bound to do, against the oversimplifications of which one can so easily be guilty in speaking of Hebrew and Greek ideas as if each was an undifferentiated monolithic entity. But, while allowing for considerable variation within each tradition, he spoke – I think quite justifiably – of a monarchical model as characteristic of the Hebrew approach to creation and of an organic model as characteristic of the Greek. Differences between different Christian doctrines of the creation he saw as derived, in part at least, from the different weight given at different times to these two traditions. He quoted with approval some words of Michael Foster which not only describe but also prescribe this dual basis for Christian doctrine: 'The Christian doctrine on this, as on all other subjects, itself includes an element derived from Greek philosophy, and any doctrine from which all Greek elements are excluded is less than Christian.'[29] Dr Macquarrie then went on to express his own conviction in these terms: 'As far as Christian theology is concerned, my thesis is that we need to move away from the monarchical model of God toward the organic model.' In other words he was consciously and deliberately advocating that the Christian doctrine of creation should move in a direction which takes it further away from the main pattern of biblical thinking. I am not here concerned with the validity or otherwise of that thesis; I am concerned with the reasons on which Dr Macquarrie bases it. These are not altogether clear. He spoke of 'the crisis of theism in the past few years' showing that the monarchical model 'has become increasingly less credible to many people today'. That could be taken to suggest a trimming of the sails of Christian doctrine to suit the limited capacity for belief of the majority of our contemporaries. I do not think his words require so pejorative an interpretation. I take it to be his conviction that a more organic model enables him to hold together in the most coherent way those things which appear to him to be true in the light both of the whole Christian tradition and of our contemporary knowledge of the way the world works. The reference to what is 'less credible to many people today' does not imply the determination of doctrine by the vote of the major-ity; if that were the case, it would be unlikely to be a Christian doctrine at all. But if something 'has become increasingly less credible to many people' it is a part of the duty of the theologian to consider why this is so; he needs to ask to what extent it is due to changes in knowledge about the world or to changes of sensibility which on mature reflection may prove to be valid. And in so far as such changes do seem to him to be valid, they must be given a place in determining his own affirmations of Christian doctrine. Certainly there is no straightforward set of criteria by which the validity of Dr Macquarrie's thesis can be tested. Its grounding and its implications would need to be developed and assessed in a wide variety of ways – as with any general thesis in, for example, the field of psychology or of moral philosophy.

The work of theology is thus a highly complex and tentative business. It is hardly surprising that a study of the way it has been done down the ages and the way it is being done today should give rise to such basic questions as: 'what is the essence of orthodoxy?' Indeed that formulation of the question is itself perhaps not basic enough. It is likely to suggest to our minds (though it does not logically imply this) that in any specific matter of doctrine there is only one right judgment to be made. Indeed it is often felt that this is a necessary condition of our being able to maintain that theological assertions are in any strong sense of the word 'objective', that true and false can properly be applied to them. But that does not seem to me to be the case. Take the analogy of the historical assessment of some complex movement from past history. It seems clear that there is not only one right way of making such an assessment. Yet it is equally clear that there are some assessments which we can properly dismiss as false.

But 'essence of orthodoxy' may suggest to us the lesser thesis that, while there may be a plurality of valid theological judg- ments, there must be some isolable inner core which will be a necessary component of all such valid judgments. But even in this form the idea does not seem to me to be necessarily true. Just as in other fields, genuine continuity of life and conviction may be compatible with a transformation of all the isolable elements which go to make up that living entity or the articulated form of that conviction. That is not to say that genuine continuity is compatible with change of any kind, but rather that the 'essence' about which we ask may turn out to be a highly elusive thing defying all our attempts to identify it and to pin it down.

Thus our relation to past Christian tradition cannot be one of identity nor even one of the preservation intact of some definable inner core of that tradition. In attempting to understand the true nature of the relation, some words of W. H. Auden with respect to the poets and artists of the twentieth century are apposite:

If we talk of tradition today, [he writes] we no longer mean what the eighteenth century meant, a way of working handed down from one generation to the next; we mean a consciousness of the whole of the past in the present. Originality no longer means a slight personal modification of one's immediate predecessors; it means the capacity to find in any other work of any date or locality clues for the treatment of one's own subject- matter.[30]

The parallel is not of course precise. The whole of the human past is relevant to the Christian theologian, but he does look to particular dates and particular localities as of supreme significance for his task in a way that the artist will not necessarily do. More-over, while there is certainly an intuitive or creative element in the work of the theologian, originality of expression is not as important an aspect of his role as it is for the artist. But the main point of the analogy holds. The theologian inherits a broad tradi-tion; without it he could not begin to do his task. It is there that he finds clues for the treatment of his own subject-matter. But he is not content simply to refurbish and modernize past statements of belief. He takes the past statements of belief with the utmost seriousness but his essential subject-matter is the contemporary world. His aim is not simply to talk about the past in the idiom of the present, but to interpret the present in the light of the past. His task cannot therefore be identified with the task of his pre-decessors and it cannot be done in precisely the same way as they did theirs.

Sometimes when I say the kind of thing that I have just said, I feel it is too obvious to need saying at all. It could be applied to any other branch of study you care to name – in science or philosophy or history we stand upon the shoulders of our predecessors, but we are not bound by their methods or their con-clusions. At other times I feel it is too revolutionary to be accept-able. For Christian theology with its firm roots in the history of Jesus and the dogmatic definitions of the church has always had a built-in fear of novelty, a desire to claim that apparent novelty was at least implicit in previous expressions of the faith.

The Christian theologian, I believe, is faced with a dual obligation. On the one hand he must be very firmly grounded in the history of the tradition. It has often been pointed out that the man who despises history is usually a slave to very recent history which he has failed to understand. That, I believe, is true of a good deal of so-called modern radical theology. On the other hand, the theologian must be prepared to challenge openly and explicitly any attempt to tie him too specifically to the ways and insights of the past; he must affirm the propriety – indeed, the necessity – of genuinely new and creative work in Christian theology.

If my emphasis has been placed on that second point, it is in no way meant to be exclusive of the former. Nothing that I have said is intended to imply the irrelevance or the unimportance of the strongly historical tradition of the Oxford Theology School; a great proportion of initial theological study must always be of that kind. It is, however, intended to call in question the adequacy of that historical tradition when, as can still happen, it is unmixed with any other elements in the student's curriculum; for while it may no longer be possible to study theology as if the world came into existence in 4004 BC, it is still possible in Oxford – by a judicious, or rather injudicious, selection of papers which is fortunately not very common – to do so as if the world went out of existence in AD 461. It is intended to call in question the propriety of allowing the philosophy of religion to remain no more than an optional element in the syllabus. The relationship of Jerusalem to Athens is an indispensable component in the study of theology, but it is not by itself sufficient. For the more deeply one studies the history of that relationship, the more clearly it emerges that our concern in theology cannot rest there alone. That concern is and must be with Jerusalem, Athens, and Oxford.

14

The Criteria of Christian Theology

Just before beginning to write this paper I read an article in *Theology*, January 1973, by Professor H. P. Owen.[1] It began by posing the problem of defining 'Christian Ethics'. For a brief, fleeting moment I thought that perhaps my task – or at least the appropriate way to tackle it – was going to be done for me. But before I had finished the first page my hopes were already dashed. For Professor Owen there declares himself 'inclined to locate the distinctive nature of Christian ethics – its differentiating factors – in its religious background (that is, in the Christian doctrines of God, Christ and human destiny).' The buck was firmly placed on the theologian's desk.

But at least it prompted me to consider whether I, as theologian, might not in turn be able to pass the buck on elsewhere. If, in the phrase 'Christian ethics', 'Christian' is not to be seen as an adjective straightforwardly qualifying the word 'ethics', with the implication that the differentiation between Christian and non-Christian ethics is not to be sought directly in differences of ethical content between them, could something similar be true also in the case of 'Christian theology'? The possibility seemed sufficiently attractive to be at least worth exploring.

How then might it be done? The most obvious possibility would seem to be to locate the distinctive nature of Christian theology – its differentiating factors – in the fact that it is theology done by Christians. That is to say that in any primary sense 'Christian' should be understood as an adjective describing certain kinds of people rather than certain sets of ideas. Only exploration of what would be involved in such a move will show whether it is a possible one – and, even if it is, whether the buck may not still land back on the theologian's table in the end.

Certainly there is little ground for thinking that criteria of a Christian person are likely to prove any easier to determine than criteria of Christian theology. But such an oblique method of approach to our subject may have its uses none the less. Reflec-tion on the question 'What is a Christian?' raises five issues that may be relevant to our enquiry.

1. If the beliefs that he holds are part of the definition of what it is to be a Christian, we are not likely to find much help in this approach. If a Christian is one who believes the Christian doctrines of God, Christ and human destiny (to use Professor Owen's phrase), then any attempt to define the Christian doc-trines held by people who are Christians will be circular to the point of vacuity. If, on the other hand, a Christian is defined as one who believes the doctrines of the Trinity, the divinity of Christ and the life to come, then we will be encouraged to look for the criteria of Christian theology in terms of its inclusion of those particular items of belief.

2. Customary usage of the term 'Christian' is remarkably varied. At one end of the scale stands a very broad, widely inclusive use of the word. At a popular level this might take the form of a defiant 'I regard myself as a Christian, even though I don't believe in God, go to church, read the gospels, etc.' As an example of a more sophisticated form one might cite Justin's description of Socrates and Heraclitus as Christians before Christ. This raises the question whether the term Christian may be used of people who have and perhaps could have had no knowledge of Jesus.

3. At the other end of the scale stands a much narrower, more exclusive use. Here one might take, as examples, the words of a devout but over-scrupulous church member, 'I wouldn't ven-ture to call myself a Christian', or, again in more sophisticated form, the insistence of Ignatius that in his martyrdom he is beginning to be a disciple and his expressed hope that he may

be found a Christian there and so merit to be called one. This prompts the reflection that what is involved in being properly called Christian may not be a matter of intellectual content only.

4. As the reference to Ignatius implies, the distinction between Christian and non-Christian may not necessarily be regarded as a straightforward either/or. It may be a matter of degree, of more or less. If we accept this approach in relation to being a Christian, we may expect it to apply also to Christian theology. It need not, however, necessarily do so since the being more or less Christian might be a matter of practice only and not affect issues of theological belief.

5. If on the other hand we do regard the distinction between Christian and non-Christian as a strict matter of either/or, we have to ask whether that distinction can be publicly known and if so by what means. If we say the distinction cannot be publicly known – either because it is a matter of election known only to God or because it is a matter of inward conversion that can be known only purely subjectively – then our enterprise is hopeless. If we say that it can be determined by some precise and public means, then the most obvious candidate for discrimination is some such criterion as being baptized and not having been formally excommunicated. This is the one line of approach that might enable the theologian to get rid of the buck in a really effective manner.

What then are the possible approaches to a search for criteria of Christian theology which these reflections suggest? 1. Can we find certain specific key beliefs which must have a place in any Christian theology? 2. Could there be a Christian theology which included no specific reference to Jesus? 3. Are some of the criteria of Christian theology of a non-intellectual character? 4. Is the distinction between Christian and non-Christian theology a matter of degree, so that we could properly speak of a theology as partly Christian? 5. Is the issue of what is a Christian theology an intellectual issue at all? Or should it be regarded as a judicial issue to be determined by ecclesiastical authority rather than by theologians? I shall set out the main body of what I want to say in the form of comment on these five approaches.

1. Can we find certain specific key beliefs which must have a place in any Christian theology?

This is not only the most natural approach to adopt; it is also that which has been most frequently adopted in Christian history. It is implicit in the insistence of the author of 1 John that the way to distinguish those who are of God from the Antichrist is whether or not they acknowledge that Jesus Christ has come in the flesh. It becomes explicit in the use of creeds as a test of orthodoxy. Nevertheless, it has serious drawbacks. Most of these are well known and I shall indicate them fairly briefly.

(*i*) In practice it is difficult to see where or why the process should stop. The author of 1 John's formula may distinguish the Christian from the docetic, but it still leaves room for Arianism. This calls for a further clarifying statement about the divine nature of the Son. Apollinarianism requires some reference to the rational soul as well as to the flesh. So too Nestorianism, Monophysitism and Monothelitism, each in turn increases the list of beliefs needed for defining what is to be accepted as Christian. If, with true Anglican moderation, I were to draw a line at the Fourth General Council, would this be more than an arbitrary decision of convenience? And if we want to work our way backward and allow Nestorian and Apollinarian theologies to be Christian, why not Arian and docetic ones too? Is it not better to see here a warning light suggesting that there may be something wrong with the whole approach with which we are working?

(*ii*) There are more important theoretical reasons which point in the same direction. To select a number of key beliefs and use them as criteria in this way is to take them out of the broader theological setting in which alone they can have a precise (indeed sometimes, any) meaning. I remember the Dean of Christ Church once beginning a course of lectures on Arianism by saying that he did not expect that there were any Arians in his audience – but that he did not expect there were any Athanasians either, for none of us held the philosophical position that was shared by them both and in terms of which alone the difference between them could properly be expressed. Paul Tillich is evidence that even so apparently essential and incontrovertible (for the Christian) a proposition as one affirming the existence of God may have some ambiguity about it in view of the different concepts of 'existence' with which a theologian may be working.

Now this kind of insistence on the culturally relative nature of theological systems and the indirect, ambiguous character of all religious language can be carried to such extremes as to render all theology cognitively vacuous. It would be absurd to suggest that the inclusion or exclusion of such beliefs as the existence of God or the coming of Jesus Christ in the flesh made no difference at all with regard to the Christian character of a proposed theology. All that is being claimed now is that they cannot function as precise criteria. In so far as they are able to function as criteria, the evidence suggests that we may need to think not in terms of black and white but of differing shades of grey. There would be nothing surprising in that. Nor would it imply that the differences between differing ends of the scale might not be very sharp indeed. But it would mean that in the middle range (which in practice, of course, are the interesting cases) there might be genuine uncertainty and that if we were to insist on a clear line of demarcation this would require a judicial decision determining what shall be deemed the point of distinction rather than an intellectual discernment perceiving the point of distinction as something already in existence. But these issues come up under our fourth and fifth headings.

2. Could there be a Christian theology which included no specific reference to Jesus?

This is an issue very much less discussed, and indeed may appear so absurd a suggestion as not to merit serious discussion. Nevertheless, it does point to an important ambiguity at the heart of Christianity which needs to be brought more clearly out into the open. This ambiguity is bound up with the word or name, Christ, itself. If we speak of 'Jesus' it is quite clear that the primary connotation of the word is a historical person, who preached in Palestine in the first century AD and was crucified under Pontius Pilate. If we speak of 'the Word' the primary connotation is slightly less easy to spell out but it is clearly a divine reality, a divine meaning or purpose, embodied according to Christian faith in the person of Jesus but not restricted to that embodiment, since (in Athanasius's words) 'the Word ... so far from being contained by anything ... rather contained all things himself.'[2] But when we come to the term 'Christ' the nature of the primary connotation is not so straightforward. We know that it was a title within Judaism (whatever the precise degree of specificity it may or may not have had there). But even within the New Testament its titular force has often disappeared and it has become little more than a name – an adjunct or alternative to Jesus. But the titular force is never wholly lost. It suggests with roughly equal immediacy divine role and historical person. This ambivalence gives it a special religious value. But it also highlights a serious theological problem.

Let me put the problem in this way. The Christ of the Fourth Gospel claims to be 'the truth' and Paul speaks of him as one 'in whom are hid all the treasures of wisdom and knowledge'. To whom are these statements to be referred? If we say 'to the Word', they are mere tautologies. If we say 'to Jesus', the implications of our claim are less clear. It might mean that all true knowledge of God derives historically from the teaching of or about Jesus, or that, however derived by us, it was in fact present to the consciousness of Jesus; or that, however derived by us, it can be shown to be consistent with the teaching of or about Jesus. Certainly Christians have normally felt the need to make some claim of this kind. Now admittedly there are very profound differences between the three samples I have given and the variety could very easily be multiplied. What they would all have in common is that everything within Christian theology would need to stand in a comparatively direct and definable relationship to the figure of Jesus. Where this is historically implausible we tend to use the title Christ and to play down in our minds the historical dimension of the word, without however allowing it to slip outside the margin of consciousness, or at least available recall, altogether. We even invent learned terms like *communicatio idiomatum* to justify our procedure to ourselves. But it seems to me that this ambiguity of reference enables the Christian theologian to practise a form of self-deception. He may in all good faith claim that his theology is strongly and clearly Christian in character because of its Christ-centredness. Yet because of the fluidity of reference of the term Christ, that Christ-centredness itself may be a highly elusive concept.

This is a very complex issue. I have done no more than hint at the nature of the problem and done little if anything to elucidate it. In relation to our immediate concerns these reflections prompt me to make the following comments. It seems to me clear that there are (and there need to be) many features in any Christian theology which do not derive in any direct way from Jesus. By sheer definition of the meaning of terms they must in any full Christian theology be brought into some sort of relation to the figure of Jesus. Nevertheless, there may well be sources of Christian theology, and even substantial subsections within a fully developed Christian theology, which will derive their material and their insights from elsewhere, including other religious traditions. Christian theology has always been far more syncretistic in practice than it has liked to admit in theory. It ought to be prepared to be more openly and honestly syncretistic.

3. Are some of the criteria of Christian theology of a non-intellectual character?

The answer, I believe, is Yes. The question, be it emphasized, is a question about criteria not about meaning. An affirmative answer to it has no direct bearing on the issue of the cognitive nature of theological statements. In all sorts of areas of knowledge – scientific, economic, etc. – the only way in which we can test the truth of our theoretical statements may be experimental. This does not mean that the procedure used for verification is to be identified with the meaning of those statements, even though it may well be the only available criterion for determining their truth.

There are two reasons why such a procedure should be expected to have a special place in relation to theology. In the first place there is the obvious impossibility of any direct checking of the truth of theological statements. Secondly there is a sense in which theology is parasitic upon the practice of religion. However much we may properly want to defend its rational or intellectual character, it is clearly rational or intellectual in a very broad sense which cannot be tied down to what we often call pejoratively purely rational or rationalistic categories without distortion.

It is therefore a perfectly proper question to ask of a theology: can it be lived by? Can it be prayed by? Eastern orthodox theologians are particularly good at asking these questions, but others should and do ask them too. Nevertheless, there are important qualifications about how we can and should ask them, and I am not sure whether, if these are properly observed, they will in fact serve as useful discriminating criteria at all. Three such qualifications are these.

(*i*) It must be clearly recognized that any such test can only be properly applied to a theology as a whole and not to individual theological statements *seriatim*. A theology can only be lived by or prayed by in a very indirect sense. A book of dietetics cannot be lived by in the same direct way as a loaf of bread, but there are situations in which it may make the greater contribution to the living standards of an undernourished people.

(*ii*) It is not to be assumed automatically that a theology in the philosophical mould cannot be lived or prayed by and that one in the biblical mould can. Pascal's dichotomy between the God of the philosophers and the God of Abraham, of Isaac and of Jacob is a grossly oversimplified one. Distinctively philosophical motifs can be developed in a fully religious way. Moreover, there can be arid scholasticism of a biblical as well as of a philosophical character.

(*iii*) For this criterion to be a criterion of Christian theology, it would have to be asked whether the theology gave rise to a Christian style of life and to a Christian kind of prayer. We are back with the problem of circularity – and even if as theologian I would not be averse to passing the buck I am certainly not prepared to pass it to the liturgiologists. I think one probably can say of some ostensibly Christian theologies that they give rise to ways of life which are bad on almost any showing (even making considerable allowance for the indirectness of the relation be-tween theology and style of life and also for the relativity of moral judgments). This I take to be the gravamen of Don Cupitt's *Crisis of Moral Authority*.[3] But clearly styles of life and forms of prayer themselves change and ought to change. It might be argued that a theology which ruled out intercessory prayer was not a genuinely Christian theology; but would a theology that ruled out any direct effect of intercessory prayer in the life of the person prayed for (i.e. other than through the enlarged sym-pathies of the person doing the praying) be justly ruled out on that ground? The difficulties of judging here are just as great as those involved in direct assessment of the Christian character of any proposed theology.

4. Is the distinction between Christian and non-Christian theologies a matter of degree, so that we could properly speak of a theology as partly Christian?

People sometimes speak as if it was only within the last few generations that Christians had woken up to the fact that God was not an old man in the sky or that there were serious philoso-phical difficulties in speaking about him. No one could have spoken more explicitly about the incomprehensibility of God, who is to be known in the darkness, than Gregory of Nyssa or John Chrysostom. But they combined this with the conviction that it was also possible on the basis of revelation to speak, for example, about the trinitarian nature of God in ways which could be declared unhesitatingly to be true, orthodox and Christian in contrast to the erroneous, heterodox and un-Christian views of the Eunomians or Macedonians. Changed attitudes to revelation and the kind of reasoning already briefly indicated under section 1. seem to me to make such a position no longer tenable.

The abandonment of such clear-cut conceptions of orthodoxy does not mean that anything goes, that since God is incomprehensible anything that may be said about him is as good as anything else. What does follow is that there are so many models with which theology may properly work – in fact with which theology needs to work in order to overcome the imbalance implicit in the use of any one model – that any assessment of the Christian character of the final product is bound to be a somewhat intuitive matter. Fixed criteria are too blunt an instrument to serve. What would be inappropriate in one context may be what needs to be said in another. Theologies must be judged as wholes and this can only be done *ad hoc* in each case.

The kind of judgment envisaged here is similar to the kind of judgment with which one might assess a psychological theory or a work of art. Even if the judgment called for was simply a judgment whether or not the work under consideration properly belonged to a certain tradition – was, let us say, Freudian or impressionist – the answer would often be: partly it does, but partly it draws creatively on quite other comparatively distinct traditions. The dominant tradition (assuming one dominant tradition to be identifiable) need not necessarily be the one (if there were one) with which the psychologist or artist consciously identified himself. If we were still to insist on a straight answer to the question whether the work was or was not Freudian or impressionist, it would have to take the form of a policy decision as to what in future was or was not to be included under the title in question. And that leads on to our fifth question.

5. Is the issue of what is a Christian theology an intellectual issue at all? Or should it be regarded as a judicial issue to be determined by ecclesiastical authority rather than by theologians?

My initial propounding of this question may have made it seem a somewhat trivial one – introduced as a bit of light relief so that I could drag in my suggestion of finally passing the buck

to ecclesiastical authority. But a good deal of the subsequent discussion has pointed towards it. In fact I am inclined to think
that of my five questions it may go farthest (even though that be
far from far) in throwing light on our problem. There are two
reasons for this. In the first place it shows that there are two
closely related but distinguishable questions, whose confusion or
premature identification greatly compounds the difficulties of the
issue. Secondly it forces us to come clean on the issue of truth.

(*i*) The two distinguishable questions which are involved in
asking about the criteria of Christian theology are: (*a*) Is this
proposed theology sufficiently in line with the historic Christian
tradition to merit the designation 'Christian'? and (*b*) Is this
proposed theology a true account of God and his relation to the
world?

Now we may believe as a matter of faith that the answers to these
two questions go together – that if we were able to answer either
one of them with a firm 'yes' or 'no', we could safely assume that
the same answer should be given to the other. Nevertheless, they
remain different questions. And it seems to me to be a part of
the risk of faith that it is at least logically possible that we might
find ourselves in a position in which we had to give different
answers to the two questions. We might find ourselves having
to say either

(*a*) I believe that what is now being proposed is true, but that
it draws so little from the Christian tradition, is so different from
what has gone by the name of Christian in the past and is
accepted by so few of those who today call themselves Christian,
that it ought not to be called a Christian theology at all, because
to do so would be to use the word 'Christian' in so Pickwickian
a sense that it would make nonsense of language as a vehicle of
public communication; or

(*b*) I believe that what is now being proposed is very close
indeed to what has been affirmed pretty consistently by the
Christian tradition throughout its history and is still affirmed by
the majority of those who call themselves Christians, but nevertheless I believe it to be false and therefore something that ought

not to be affirmed by Christians or by anyone else. This would not imply the death of Christian theology, provided there were something else that could be affirmed as true, which, even if nowhere near as close to earlier affirmations of the Christian tradition, was yet sufficiently consistent with that tradition to merit the designation 'Christian' in a non-Pickwickian sense.

But the heart of the problem is still of course firmly with us. When is the word 'Christian' being used in a Pickwickian sense? And if this is an issue which calls for judicial decision who is to do the deciding and how?

It would not be a free policy decision in the hands of ecclesiastical authority, in the sense that they could decide, for example, that as from 1 January 1974 a Christian theology would be one that coincided with the teaching of the Quran or the writings of Karl Marx. Even in the unlikely event that this gave rise to no splinter groups claiming the name of continuing Christians for themselves, it would still be illegitimate. Part of the meaning of a word is what it has meant in the past, and non-Christians would have some (if lesser) rights in relation to the issue. The position of the ecclesiastical authorities is more like that of trustees. They would not be free to do whatever they chose. They would have to show that in doing what they did they were behaving reasonably and responsibly in relation to the past. This would involve an appeal to criteria other than the mere *fiat* of their own decision. But I do not see how such criteria could be other than of a very general character and I am doubtful how clear would be the guidance they would provide in any case of serious interest, which would by definition be a borderline case and not like the absurd and absurdly obvious case that I have invented for the sake of illustration. There would always be considerable latitude within which a reasonable and responsible decision might perfectly well go either way with equally cogent arguments on either side.

(*ii*) This question – is a position properly to be called Christian? – is subsidiary to the question, Is it true? Chronologically they may arise in either order. I may be convinced of the truth of some theological position and then, as a second question, go on to ask whether it can properly be called Christian. Or heuristically I may ask what in the light of Christian tradition might be a proper Christian theological position on some particular issue today. This approach may well suggest certain possibilities which would not have occurred to me had I not explicitly posed the question in that way with a conscious reference back to the Christian tradition. But that does nothing to relieve me of the responsibility of asking as a genuinely open question whether or not that position is true.

It is not possible within the compass of this comparatively brief paper to embark on a discussion of how one is to determine whether or not a theological position is true. I am assuming that it does make sense (even if not a simple or straightforward sense) to speak of theological positions as true or false, and that, however complex and difficult the procedures involved, it is a question not only worth asking but also worth trying to answer. What I have been primarily trying to show is the relationship between that question and the other question, 'Is it Christian?'

What then are the criteria of Christian theology? I have not found myself able to propose any set of beliefs, or other distinguishing characteristics, which any Christian theology must include or exclude. This does not seem to me to be a matter of very great importance. I would want to suggest that any theology that emerges out of a serious attention to the Christian tradition has a *prima facie* claim to being considered a Christian theology. The important issue that then arises is not whether its *prima facie* claim to be called Christian is sound or not, but whether or not it is true. Whether, for example, a death of God theology which gives a focal place to Jesus has or has not a right to be called Christian is not an issue worth discussing, until we have independently assessed its truth claims. If a position of that kind which has clear links with the historic Christian tradition but also very sharp differences from it does arise and provides us with grounds for believing it to be true, that is the moment at which we will find ourselves faced with the need to assess whether or not it is to be regarded as a Christian theology. There will very often be a roughly even case to be made out on either side, and a decision may be called for of a kind of which it does not make sense to ask whether it is 'right' or 'wrong'. We ought not to underestimate either the extent of the shifts that have taken place in what is regarded as a Christian theology down the ages or the creative character of the conciliar decisions or more gradual processes of change by which those shifts have been effected. We cannot now foresee or foreclose where such shifts may take us in the future.

I would claim that such an approach does not undermine the truth claims of Christian theology. In fact it rather underlines them. But at the same time it leaves room, as I believe room must be left, for a plurality of theologies both within and without Christianity. Yet it is precisely the conviction that these two things are necessarily in conflict with one another that is the source of so much contemporary anxiety on this whole issue.

NOTES

1. Some Reflections on the Origins of the Doctrine of the Trinity
Journal of Theological Studies, new series, VIII, 1957, pp. 92–106.

1. L. Hodgson, *Doctrine of the Trinity*, Nisbet 1943, p.25.
2. Ibid., p.229.
3. J. F. Bethune-Baker, *Introduction to the Early History of Christian Doctrine* (5th ed. 1933), p.106.
4. Irenaeus, *Demonstratio*, 45.
5. Novatian, *De Trinitate*, 17, 18.
6. Tertullian, *Adversus Praxeam*, 15.
7. Irenaeus, op. cit., 47.
8. John 1.2; Col. 1.16.
9. Origen, *De Principiis*, i. 3. 5 (Greek text preserved by Justinian, *Ep. ad Mennam*, Mansi, ix. 524).
10. For examples see pp.8–9 below. The famous saying 'where the church is, there is the Spirit of God, and where the Spirit of God is, there is the church and all grace' (*Adversus Haereses* iii. 24. 1) appears to make Irenaeus' view agree closely with that of Origen. The context, however, makes it quite clear that it is not intended as a complete description of the sphere of the Spirit's activity, but simply to deny his operation in heretical bodies.
11. Cf. for example, Gregory of Nyssa: 'The Holy Spirit, from whom all the supply of good things for the creation has its source' (printed among the letters of Basil as *Ep.* 38.4).
12. Cf. Novatian, *De Trin.*, 29: 'The Holy Spirit is not new in the Gospel, nor yet even newly given, for it was He Himself who accused the people in the prophets.'
13. In A. E. J. Rawlinson (ed.), *Essays on the Trinity and the Incarnation* (1928).
14. Rawlinson, op. cit., p.227.
15. Ibid., p.234.

16. Justin, *Apologia* i. 33; Tertullian, *Adv. Prax.*, 26; *De Carne Christi*, 14.

17. E.g., Hippolytus, *Contra Noetum*, 4; Lactantius, *Div. Inst.*, iv. 12.

18. J. Armitage Robinson, *St. Irenaeus: Demonstratio* (1920), p.67. (Cf. Irenaeus, *Adv. Haer.*, iii. 21.4; v. 1.3; *Dem.*, 40, 71.)

19. Cf. G. Dix, *The Shape of the Liturgy*, A. & C. Black 1944, p.276; G. Kretschmar, *Studien zur frühchristlichen Trinitätstheologie*, Tübingen, pp.190, 191.

20. Justin, *Ap.*, i. 6, 13.

21. Ibid., 61.

22. Irenaeus, *Dem.*, 100.

23. *Adv. Haer.*, i. 10.1.

24. Justin, *Ap.*, i. 31, 44 and 36.

25. Irenaeus, *Adv. Haer.*, iv. 20.4, 8.

26. Hippolytus, *Con. Noet.*, 11, 12.

27. H. Lietzmann, *Geschichte der alten Kirche*, ii (1936), p.184: English translation, 'Founding of the Church Universal', *A History of the Early Church* II, Lutterworth 1961, p.184.

28. H. B. Swete, article 'Holy Ghost' in W. Smith and H. Wace (eds), *Dictionary of Christian Biography*, 1882, iii, p.118.

29. J. Lawson, *Biblical Theology of St. Irenaeus*, Epworth 1948, p.127.

30. Irenaeus, *Adv. Haer.*, ii, 28.2; iv. 20.6.

31. *Dem.*, 5–7.

32. Eusebius, *Dem. Ev.*, iv. 13.2, 3 (cf. Irenaeus, *Adv. Haer.*, ii. 2.4, 5).

33. Athenagoras, *Supplicatio*, vi. 3.

34. Irenaeus, *Dem.*, 5.

35. *Adv. Haer.*, iii. 24.2.

36. Ibid., iv. 20.2.

37. Ibid., iv. 38.3.

38. Hippolytus, *Con. Noet.*, 10.

39. G. L. Prestige, *God in Patristic Thought*, SPCK 1952, p.36.

40. Irenaeus, *Dem.*, 5.

41. Tertullian, *Adv. Herm.*, 45 (cf. also *Adv. Prax.*, 7, 19).

42. Theophilus, *Ad Aut.*, ii. 15; (cf. also ibid., i. 7; ii. 10).

43. Irenaeus, *Adv. Haer.*, iv. 7.4; iv. 20.3; *Dem.*, 5, 10.

44. Athenagoras, *Suppl.*, xxiv. 1; Tertullian, *Adv. Prax.*, 6, 19; Origen, *De Princ.*, i. 2.3; i. 2.10; ii. 9.4; *Comm. Jn*, i. 19.

45. E. F. Scott, *The Spirit in the New Testament*, 1923, p.232.

46. See p.6 above.

47. Irenaeus, *Dem.*, 6, 7.

48. Origen, *Hom. Ex.*, viii. 4.

49. Tertullian, *Adv. Prax.*, 26 (cf. also Hippolytus, *Con. Noet.*, 14).

50. Origen, *De Princ.*, i. 3 .2.

51. See p.6 above (cf. also *Adv. Haer.*, iv. 33 .7).

52. Origen, *De Princ.*, praef. 2, 4 (cf. also *Matt. Comm. Ser.*, 33; *Comm. Jn*, xxxii. 16; *Hom. Jer.*, v. 13; *I Cor. Frag.*, 4, in *Journal of Theological Studies*, IX, 1908, p.234.

53. Tertullian, *Adv. Prax.*, 2; *De Praescriptione*, 13.

54. See Kelly, *Early Christian Creeds*, especially pp.23–29, 94.

55. Origen, *Hom. Num.*, xii. 1.

56. Printed among the letters of Basil as *Ep.*, 189 .6, 7.

57. E.g., Athanasius, *Ad Serapionem*, i. 14, 20; Basil, *De Spiritu Sancto*, 19; ps-Basil (probably Didymus), *Adv. Eun.*, iv. 1. (*Patrologia Graeca* ed. J.-P. Migne (*PG*) 29: 676A); Gregory of Nyssa, *Contra Eunomium*, ii (*PG* 45: 564A, B); Didymus, *De Spir. Sanct.*, 16; Cyril of Alexandria, *Comm. Jn*, in vi. 45 (*PG* 73: 556), in xiv. 14 (*PG* 74: 249C–252B), in xv. 1 (*PG* 74: 333D–337D).

58. Cyril, *Catecheses*, xvi. 24; Athanasius, *Ad Ser.*, i. 28, 21; Gregory of Nyssa, *Quod non sint tres dei* (*PG* 45: 125C); Cyril Alex., *Comm. Jn*, in vi. 57 (*PG* 73: 588A).

59. Rufinus, *Com. in Symb. Ap.*, 10 (cf. Athanasius, *Ad Ser.*, iii. 6).

60. Cyril Alex., *Comm. Jn*, in vi. 57 (*PG* 73: 585D–588A).

61. Athanasius, *Ad Ser.*, i. 31, iii. 5; Didymus, *De Spir. Sanct.*, 29, *De Trin.*, ii (*PG* 39: 500); Cyril Alex., *De Trin.*, vii (*PG* 75: 1093C–1096A).

62. Athanasius, *Ad Ser.*, iii. 5.

63. Basil, *De Spir. Sanct.*, 38; Gregory Nazianzen, *Orationes*, xxxviii. 9 (cf. Gregory of Nyssa, *Adv. Mac.*, 13).

64. Basil, *Adversus Eunomium*, iii. 5; Eunomius, *Apology*, 27; Gregory of Nyssa, *Adv. Mac.*, 11; ps-Athanasius, *De Trin.*, iii. 16–19.

65. Didymus, *De Trin.*, ii (*PG* 39: 565C).

66. Basil, *De Spir. Sanct.*, v. 7–12; Gregory Nazianzen, *Or.*, xxxi. 20; xxxix. 12.

67. Basil, *Epistle*, 214 .4; 236 .6.

68. Gregory Nazianzen, *Or.*, xxxi. 8 (a large number of examples are listed in K. Holl, *Amphilocius von Ikonium* (1904), pp.167–8).

69. Gregory of Nyssa, *Con. Eun.*, i (*PG* 45: 336B–D); cf. also *Adv. Mac.*, 2.

70. This is most forcefully expressed by Gregory of Nyssa, *De Com. Not.* (*PG* 45: 180C); *Adv. Mac.*, 14; *De Fide* (*PG* 45: 144A, B). Cf. also Gregory Nazianzen, *Or.*, xxix. 16; xxxi. 9. It should be noticed that even the division of the activity of the Trinity in the work of creation already quoted (see pp.12–13 above) is really inconsistent with this insistence on the complete identity of their operations. There is no doubt that it is the latter which is their main teaching. (Cf. K. Holl, op. cit., pp.146–7.)

71. E.g., Augustine, *De Trin.*, iv. 30.

72. Athanasius, *Ad Ser.*, iv. 3–6.

73. Gregory Nazianzen, *Or.*, xxix. 16; xxxi. 9; Basil, *De Spir. Sanct.*, 24–28.

74. Karl Barth, *Kircheliche Dogmatik*, 1/1 (1932), pp.395, 381–2; English translation, *The Doctrine of the Word of God*, T. & T. Clark 1936, pp.430, 415. C. R. Welch, *The Trinity in Contemporary Theology*, SCM Press 1953, pp.192–3.

75. Welch, op. cit., pp.168–71 (cf. also L. Hodgson's criticism of the view in *Journal of Theological Studies*, new series, V, 1954, p.50).

76. Barth, op. cit., pp.382–3 (English translation pp. 416–17).

77. Welch, op. cit., p.223.

78. Hippolytus, *Con. Noet.*, 14.

79. Thomas Aquinas, *Summa Theologiae*, i, Q.32.1.

80. Ibid., Q.32.3.

81. Ibid., Q.40.1.

82. D. M. Edwards, *Christianity and Philosophy* (1932), pp.339, 354, 355.

2. Eternal Generation

Journal of Theological Studies, new series, XII, 1961, pp.284–91

1. Tatian, *Or. ad Graec.*, 5.

2. Theophilus, *Ad Aut.*, ii. 10, 22.

3. Ibid., 22; Athenagoras, *Suppl.*, x.

4. Justin, *Dial. with Trypho*, 61, 129.

5. Ibid., 63.

6. Hippolytus, *Con. Noet.*, 15.

7. G. L. Prestige, *God in Patristic Thought*, pp.37–54.

8. Ibid., p.149.

9. L. Hodgson, *Doctrine of the Trinity*, p.100.

10. Cf. also Origen, *De Princ.*, i. 2.4; iv. 4.1.

11. Justin, *Dial.*, 128; Tatian, *Or. ad Graec.*, 5; Hippolytus, *Con. Noet.*, 10 and 11.

12. Justin, *Dial.*, 128

13. Eusebius, *Dem. Ev.*, iv. 3.7.

14. Origen, *De Princ.*, i. 2.2.

15. Ibid., i. 2.10; i. 4.3; iii. 5.3.

16. Daniélou, *Origène*, Paris 1948, p.253. English translation, *Origen*, Sheed & Ward 1955, p.256.

17 Athanasius, *De Sent. Dion.*, 15.

18. Novatian, *De Trin.*, 31.

19. Origen, *De Princ.*, i. 2.10.

20. Athanasius, *De Decr.*, 20; *Ad Afros*, 5.

21. Id., *Or. Con. Ar.*, iii. 28.

22. Methodius, *De Creatis*, 2–5.

23. Athanasius, *Or. Con. Ar.*, i. 29.

24. Ibid., 28.

25. Ibid., iii. 66.

26. Athanasius, *De Decr.*, 15; *Or. Con. Ar.*, i. 14, 19; ii. 32.

27. Origen, *De Princ.*, iv. 4.1. Cf. also, for Dionysius, Athanasius, *De Sent. Dion.*, 15.

28. Origen, *Comm. Jn*, ii. 23.

29. See Jerome, *Ep. ad Avitum*, 2.

30. In the coequal Trinity, reason, wisdom, and power are in no sense exclusive properties of the second person of the Trinity and therefore the denial of the coeternity of the Son would not involve the implication that the Father was once without reason, wisdom or power. Cf. R. C. Moberly, *Atonement and Personality* (1907), pp.172 and 206–7.

3. In Defence of Arius

Journal of Theological Studies, new series, XIII, 1962, pp.339–47.

1. H. M. Gwatkin, *Studies in Arianism*[2] (1882), p.274.

2. 'Logos and Son in Origen, Arius and Athanasius', *Studia Patristica*, ii (*Texte und Untersuchungen*, lxiv), pp.282–7; 'The Origins of Arianism', *Journal of Theological Studies*, new series, IX, 1958, pp.103–11.

3. Pollard, 'The Origins of Arianism', p.110; Gwatkin, op. cit., p.2.

4. Pollard, art. cit., pp.105–6.

5. J. Quasten, *Patrology*, ii, p.114; L. B. Radford, *Three Teachers of Alexandria: Theognostus, Pierius and Peter*, pp.58–86.

6. Procopius, *Commentarius in Genesim*, iii. 21 (*PG* 87. 1: 221B).

7. The date of Peter's martyrdom was 24 November 311 (not 310); that of Lucian was 7 January 312.

8. See W. Telfer, 'St Peter of Alexandria and Arius', *Analecta Bollandiana*, lxvii (1949), pp.117–30.

9. Pollard, *Studia Patristica*, ii, p.287.

10. Origen, *De Princ.*, iv. 4.1.

11. *Comm. Jn*, i. 24, 38.

12. Athanasius, *Contra Gentes*, 41.

13. *Or. Con. Ar.*, ii. 34.

14. Pollard, 'The Origins of Arianism', p.106.

15. Origen, *De Princ.*, i. 1.6 (see G. W. Butterworth, *Origen on First Principles*, 1936, p.10, note ad loc.).

16. *Comm. Jn*, i. 20.

17. Pollard, art. cit., pp.106–7.

18. Origen, *De Princ.*, iv. 4.8,

19. *Comm. Jn*, ii. 2.

20. *Contra Celsum*, v. 4.

21. Ibid., v. 11; *Exhort. Mart.*, 7.

22. *Comm. Jn*, ii. 23; xiii. 3.

23. Ibid., i. 21.

24. 'Thalia' in Athanasius, *De Synodis*, 15: ἐπινοεῖται γοῦν μυρίαις ὅσαις ἐπινοίαις πνεῦμα, δύναμις, σοφία, δόξα θεοῦ, ἀλήθεία τε καὶ εἰκὼν καὶ λόγος οὗτος.

25. Origen, *Comm. Jn*, xiii. 25.

26. *Comm. Matt.*, xv. 10; cf. also *Con. Cels.*, v. 11.

27. J. F. Bethune-Baker, *An Introduction to the Early History of Christian Doctrine*, p.160.

28. Pollard, 'The Origins of Arianism', p.110.

29. Origen, *De Princ.*, iv. 4.1; Theognostus in Photius, *Bibl. Cod.*, 106. It is instructive to observe the way in which the discussion of this issue is frequently conducted by modern authors. Thus J. F. Bethune-Baker (op. cit., p.148, n.2) writes, 'Origen certainly never meant it in any Arian sense'; and L. B. Radford (op. cit., p.14) writes, 'The Arian sense of the word κτίσμα is ruled out of consideration in this case by the appeal which

Athanasius makes as against the Arians to "the learned Theognostus" '.
Both writers assume that there is a clear-cut and well-known 'Arian sense'
of the word κτίσμα whose significance and interpretation allows of no
doubt or discussion.

30. Athanasius, *De Sent. Dion.*, 18.

31. Letter to Paulinus of Tyre; Opitz, *Urkunden zur Geschichte des
Arianischen Streites* (*Athanasius Werke*, Bd. III, teil 1), Document viii. 4–7.

32. Letter to Alexander of Alexandria (Opitz, op. cit., Document vi. 3).

33. The phrase is taken from I. T. Ramsey, *Religious Language*, SCM
Press 1957, ch. 2. It should be added that Professor Ramsey does not take
such a favourable view of Arius's understanding of theological method as
I do (op. cit., p.159).

34. Athanasius, *Or. Con. Ar.*, i. 5 and 37; Arius, Letter to Alexander
of Alexandria (Opitz, op. cit., Document vi. 2).

35. Both terms are included in the ἐπινοίαι of the Son referred to in the
'Thalia' (Athanasius, *De Synodis*, 15).

36. As is done by Gwatkin, op. cit., p.76, n.2.

37. Pollard, *Studia Patristica*, ii, art. cit., p.287.

38. Athanasius, *De Syn.*, 51.

39. See especially R. V. Sellers, *Two Ancient Christologies*, SPCK 1954,
pp.116–17.

4. The Doctrine of Christ in the Patristic Age

Originally read as a paper for the Fiftieth Annual Conference of Modern
Churchmen July 1967 under the chairmanship of Dr Norman Pittenger.
Published in *Christ for Us Today*, SCM Press 1968, pp.81–90.

5. The Nature of the Early Debate about Christ's Human Soul
Journal of Ecclesiastical History, XVI, no. 2, 1965, pp.139–51.

1. Justin, *Ap.*, ii. 10.

2. C. E. Raven, *Apollinarianism*, Cambridge 1923, p.12.

3. E. R. Goodenough, *Theology of Justin Martyr*, Jena 1923, p.240.

4. Irenaeus, *Adv. Haer.*, v. 1, 1.

5. Tertullian, *De Carne Christi*, xvi.

6. *De Resurrectione Carnis*, ii.

7. *De Carne Christi*, x.

8. *De Res. Carn.*, xxxiv.

9. *De Carne Christi*, xiii.

10. Hippolytus, *Con. Noet.*, xvii.

11. Victorinus, *Adv. Ar.*, iii. 3; iv. 7 (*Patrologia Latina*, ed. J.-P. Migne (*PL*), viii. 1100D–1101A; 1118A); Hilary, *De Trin.*, x. 19; 50–60 (*PL*, x. 357; 383–90).

12. Novatian, *De Trin.*, xxv.

13. J. N. D. Kelly, *Early Christian Doctrines*, A. & C. Black 1958 p.153.

14. A. d'Alès, *Novatien*, Paris 1924, p.108.

15. But see n. 27 below.

16. Origen, *Dialogue with Herakleides*, ed. J. Scherer, Cairo 1949, p.136. A more detailed study of this subject would have to distinguish carefully between writers who think in trichotomist terms and, indeed, between differing usages within the writings of a single author. But the distinction is not of vital importance in a general treatment of the kind being undertaken here. The issue at stake does not really concern the animal soul at all; it is whether there was in Jesus a human element fulfilling a reasoning, guiding and determining function, by whatever name it may be described.

17. *De Princ.*, ii. 8 . 4; iv. 4 .4; ii. 8 .1.

18. *Comm. Jn*, ii. 26.

19. *De Princ.*, ii. 6 .5.

20. Ibid., iv. 4 .5; *Con. Cels.*, iv. 18 (see also *Con. Cels.*, iv. 15, where the application is to the divine Word and clearly no conflict is felt with the other application in *Con. Cels.*, iv. 18).

21. See G. W. Butterworth, *Origen on First Principles*, 1936, p.320, n. 1.

22. Origen, *De Princ.*, ii. 6 .3.

23. H. de Riedmatten, *Les Actes du Procès de Paul de Samosate*, Fribourg 1952, pp.145, 147, 155 (Frags. no. 19, 24, 33).

24. Ibid., pp.156–7 (Frag. no. 36).

25. Ibid., p.154 (Frag. no. 30).

26. Pamphilus, *Apologia pro Origene*, v (*PG*, xvii. 590AB).

27. A. Grillmeier, *Das Konzil von Chalkedon*, i., Würzburg 1951, pp.80–1; H. de Riedmatten, op. cit., pp.62–7. The most interesting single example is the passage where Methodius takes over the interpretation which Origen had given to Psalm xlv in terms of the soul of Christ and reapplies

it to the flesh of Christ: *Symposium*, vii. 8. It can, however, be legitimately argued that this may have been determined by the concern of the context with the question of virginity and is not decisive as evidence concerning Methodius's belief about Christ's human soul. De Riedmatten includes Novatian amongst those who are illustrative of this late third-century way of thought. I have earlier argued that he is, perhaps, more easily understood in the light of the otherwise unanimous tradition of Western thought. His own writings do not seem to me conclusive in either direction. If he was influenced by the Greek-speaking writers of his own day, then de Riedmatten's interpretation (with which Kelly so strongly agrees) may be correct.

28. H. de Riedmatten, op. cit., pp.68–81.

29. Ibid., p.78, n. 75, where detailed references are given.

30. Origen, *De Princ.*, ii. 8.5.

31. Epiphanius, *Ancoratus*, xxxv.

32. H. de Riedmatten, op. cit., p.113.

33. Athanasius, *Or. Con. Ar.*, iii. 26.

34. A. Grillmeier, op. cit., pp.77–102; M. Richard, *S. Athanase et la psychologie du Christ selon les Ariens* (Mélanges de Science Religieuse 1947), iv, pp.5–54. The various attempts to refute Richard's contentions do not seem to me to have shaken his position. For a discussion of the recent controversy on this topic, see A. Gesché, 'L'âme humaine de Jesus dans la Christologie du IVe siècle', *Revue d'Histoire Ecclesiastique*, LIV, 1959, pp.385–90, 403–9.

35. M. Spannuet, *Recherches sur les Écrits d'Eustathe d'Antioche*, Lille 1948, p.108 (Frag. no. 41).

36. Tertullian, *Adv. Prax.*, 27.

37. Origen, *Comm. Jn*, i. 28.

38. Cf. Athanasius, *Or. Con. Ar.*, iii. 30: 'The Word became man, and did not come into man'.

39. It should be made quite clear that I use the term 'soteriological' here to refer to the argument that Christ must have had a human soul for our human souls to be saved by him. It should not be understood to deny the very important truth that Athanasius's misgivings about the measure of unity implicit in a Word-man christology were also motivated by soteriological concerns.

40. E.g., Eustathius, Frag. no. 17 (M. Spannuet, op. cit., p. 100).

41. Athanasius, *Ad Epictetum*, vii.

42. Apollinarius, *Ep. ad Dion.*, i. (H. Lietzmann, *Apollinaris von Laodicea und seine Schule*, Tübingen 1904, pp.256–7).

43. Lietzmann, op. cit., p.204 (Frag. no. 2).

44. Ibid., p.222 (Frag. no. 76); p.276 (*Ep ad Diocaes.*, ii). The difficulty raised here by Apollinarius had been felt long before by Origen. Origen not only noted that the term 'soul' is far more often the object of censure than of praise in Scripture, but even tentatively derived the word ψυχή from ψύχεσθαι (to grow cold) on the ground that it is something which has fallen away from its original and intended warmth of love towards that which is divine (*De Princ.*, ii. 8. 3). With such an approach to the idea of the soul, it is hardly surprising that Origen should have recognized that the ascription of a human soul to Christ might seem strange to some. He himself dealt with the difficulty in terms of his own peculiar doctrine of the pre-existence of souls by claiming that Christ's soul was unique in having clung to the Logos without the slightest deviation of love or purpose (ibid., ii. vi. 5). A Gesché has pointed out that when the author of the *Commentary on the Psalms* discovered at Tura (probably Didymus) deals with this objection of Apollinarius, he does so in a way which probably derives from his close acquaintance with the thought of Origen: art. cit., pp.421–3; *La Christologie du 'Commentaire des Psaumes' découvert à Taura*, Gembloux 1962, pp.140–8.

45. Gregory Nazianzen, *Ep.*, ci. 7.

46. Ps-Athanasius, *De Incarnatione Contra Apollinarem*, i. 17.

47. A. Gesché, op. cit., p.123.

48. Ibid., pp.304, 321, 405–6.

49. Ibid., pp.147, 211, 358.

50. Dr Kelly has argued that Christ's human soul plays a more active role in the thought of Cyril after the Nestorian controversy. Nevertheless, the modification in Cyril's later thought to which he points does not seem sufficient to undermine the general contrast with the Antiochene approach described here (op. cit., p.323).

6. *The Theological Legacy of St Cyprian*

Journal of Ecclesiastical History, XIV, no. 2, 1963, pp.139–49. Originally read as a paper to the Oxford Society of Historical Theology.

1. W. D. Niven, 'Cyprian of Carthage', *Expository Times*, XLIV, 1932–3, p.363.

2. A. d'Alès, *La Théologie de S. Cyprien*, Paris 1922.

3. O. D. Watkins, *A History of Penance* (1920), p.177.

4. Pontius, *Vita Cypriani*, 2.

5. Cyprian, *Ad Donatum*, 4.

6. J. B. Lightfoot, *St Paul's Epistle to the Philippians* (1868), p.258.

7. See especially M. Simon, 'Le Judaisme berbère dans l'Afrique ancienne', *Revue d'histoire et de philosophie religieuses*, XXVI, 1946, pp.1–31, 105–45.

8. R. P. C. Hanson, 'Notes on Tertullian's Interpretation of Scripture', *Journal of Theological Studies*, new series, XII, 1961, pp.273–9.

9. Cyprian, *Epistle*, lxix. 12.

10. *Ep.*, lxiv. 2–4.

11. *Ep.*, lxvii. 4.

12. *Ep.*, i. 1.

13. *Epp.*, iii. 1; iv. 4; xxxix. 7; lix. 4; lxvi. 3.

14. *Epp.*, iii, 1; lxvii. 3; lxix. 9; *De Unitate Catholicae Ecclesiae*, xvii–xviii.

15. *Epp.*, lxv. 2; lxvii. 1; lxxii. 2.

16. Justin, *Ap.*, i. 66.

17. *Dial. with Trypho*, cxvii.

18. Ibid., xli. 3; Irenaeus, *Adv. Haer.*, iv. 18, 4.

19. Cyprian, *Ep.*, lxiii. 9, 17.

7. One Baptism for the Remission of Sins
Church Quarterly Review, CLXV, 1964, pp.59–66.

1. Cf. C. F. D. Moule, *Worship in the New Testament*, Lutterworth 1961, p.57.

2. Justin, *Ap.*, i, 61.

3. Cf. Moule, op. cit., pp.59–60

4. Hermas, *Mandates*, 4, 3, 1.

5. Tertullian, *De Baptismo*, 18.

6. Clement Alex., *Quis Dives*, 40.

7. *Stromateis*, 4, 154, 3.

8. Origen, *Comm. in Rom. iii. 28* (ed. J. Scherer, p.164); *Comm. in Rom. 3, 9* (PG 953C).

9. Fragment on I Cor., 5. 9–11 (*Journal of Theological Studies* IX, 1907–8, p.366).

10. *Mandates*, 12, 6, 2.

11. Cyprian, *Ep.*, 16.2; *De Op. et El.*, 2.

12. Origen, *Hom. in Lev.*, 2. Cf. W. Telfer, *Forgiveness of Sins*, SCM Press 1959, p.57.

13. *Similitudes*, 7, 4.

14. Tertullian, *De Poenitentia*, 9.

15. 2 Clem. 16.

16. Cyprian, *Ep.*, 55.22. The main text upon which the propitiatory efficacy of almsgiving was based is Luke 11.41, but in seeking wider scriptural backing Cyprian makes extensive use of Tobit and the Wisdom literature generally (*De Op. et El.*, 5 and 20; *Testimonia*, 3.1).

17. J. N. D. Kelly, *Early Christian Creeds*, p. 384.

18. I Tim. 1.13.

19. E.g., Shepherd of Hermas, *Similitudes*, 5, 7, 3; 9, 18, 1; Tertullian, *De Poenitentia*, 5.

20. J. H. Newman, *Doctrine of Development* (1878), pp.381ff.

21. A. d'Alès, *La théologie de S. Cyprien*, Paris 1922, p.31.

22. J. Knox, *The Ethic of Jesus in the Teaching of the Church*, Epworth 1962, pp.75ff.

8. The Consequences of Modern Understanding of Reality for the Relevance and Authority of the Tradition of the Early Church in our Time

Oecumenica, 1971/2, pp.130–43. Originally read as a paper at a consultation of Anglican and Lutheran theologians at the Institute for Ecumenical Research, Strasbourg, in March 1970. The other papers read on that occasion, including the Lutheran contribution on the same subject by Dr Ragnar Holte, are printed in the same volume of *Oecumenica*.

1. J. M. Creed, *The Divinity of Jesus Christ*, Cambridge 1938, p.106'

2. N. P. Williams, 'What is Theology?' in K. E. Kirk (ed.), *The Study of Theology* (1930), pp.67, 71.

3. C. Gore, *The Incarnation of the Son of God* (1909), p.105.

4. I have already developed the argument very briefly outlined here more fully in my first chapter: 'Some Reflections on the Origins of the Doctrine of the Trinity'.

5. See article on 'Jesus Christ', in *Sacramentum Mundi*, Herder 1968, vol. 3, p.196.

9. The Unassumed is the Unhealed

Religious Studies, 4, 1968, pp.47–56. Originally read as a paper to the Society for the Study of Theology meeting at Oxford in March 1968.

1. Barth, *Church Dogmatics*, I, 2, p.32.
2. Origen, *Con. Cels.*, iv. 19.
3. Athanasius, *Or. Con. Ar.*, iii. 31.
4. Gregory of Nyssa, *Oratio Catechetica Magna*, 27.

10. Does Christology Rest on a Mistake?

Religious Studies, 6, 1970, pp.69–76. Originally read as a paper to the Theological Teachers' Group in the University of London, May 1969.

1. P. G. Fothergill, 'Evolution' in *A Catholic Dictionary of Theology*, 1967, vol. II, pp.259–60.
2. Aubrey Moore, cited by A. R. Vidler, *The Church in an Age of Revolution*, Penguin 1961, p.121.
3. J. S. Whale, *Christian Doctrine*, CUP 1941, p.49: cited by F. W. Dillistone, 'The Fall: Christian Truth and Literary Symbol', in *Comparative Literature Studies*, vol. II, no. 4, 1965, p.359.
4. E. L. Mascall, *Theology and the Future*, Darton, Longman & Todd 1968, pp.105–6.

11. Religious Authority and Divine Action

Religious Studies, 7, 1971, pp.1–12. Originally given as a public lecture in the University of Manchester.

1. Otto Küster, cited by H. Zahrnt, *The Question of God*, Collins 1969, p.246.
2. Cf. H. W. Bartsch (ed.), *Kerygma and Myth*, SPCK 1953, vol. I, pp.197, 198–9.
3. *Anglican Theological Review*, vol. 47, January 1965, pp. 66–80.Cf. also L. B. Gilkey, 'Cosmology, Ontology and the Travail of Biblical Language', *Journal of Religion*, vol. 41, July 1961, pp.194–205.
4. Dilley, art. cit., p.78.
5. C. W. Kegley (ed.), *The Theology of Rudolph Bultmann*, SCM Press 1966, p.122.
6. D. D. Williams, 'How does God act?: an essay in Whitehead's

metaphysics' in W. L. Reese and E. Freeman (eds), *Process and Divinity*, Lasalle, Il., 1964.

7. P. Baelz, *Prayer and Providence*, SCM Press 1968, pp.81–2.

8. Aquinas, *Summa Theologiae*, 1a, 13, 7.

9. S. Ogden, *The Reality of God*, SCM Press 1967, p.180.

10. J. L. Ice and J. J. Carey (eds), *The Death of God Debate*, Westminster Press 1967, p.223.

12. Looking into the Sun

Church Quarterly, 1, no. 3, January 1969, pp. 191–201. An inaugural lecture in the Chair of Christian Doctrine in the University of London delivered in January 1968.

1. *Babylonian Talmud*, Hullin 59b–60a.

2. J. Smart (ed.), *Revolutionary Theology in the Making: Barth – Thurneysen Correspondence 1914–25*, John Knox Press 1964, pp.92–3.

3. S. Neill, *The Interpretation of the New Testament 1861–1961*, OUP 1963, p.31.

4. R. E. Prothero, *Life and Letters of Dean Stanley* (1893), vol. 2, p.170.

5. Second Visitation Charge in the Diocese of Oxford, 1893; cited by G. W. H. Lampe, 'The Bible since the Rise of Critical Study', in *The Church's Use of the Bible*, ed. D. E. Nineham, SPCK 1963.

6. F. G. Healey (ed.), *Prospect for Theology*, Nisbet 1966, pp.73–92.

7. Rahner, *Theological Investigations*, vol. 5, Darton, Longman & Todd 1966, pp.157–92.

8. *Grundzüge der Christologie*, Gütersloh 1964, p.79. English translation, *Jesus – God and Man*, SCM Press 1968, p.83. Cited by G. G. O'Collins, 'The Christology of Wolfhart Pannenberg', *Religious Studies*, 3, 1967, p.371.

9. H. M. Rumscheidt, in *Scottish Journal of Theology*, 18, 1965, p.489; cited by O'Collins, art. cit., p.375.

13. Jerusalem, Athens and Oxford

An inaugural lecture delivered before the University of Oxford in May 1971.

1. Cited by E. Molland, *The Conception of the Gospel in Alexandrian Theology*, Oslo 1938, p.170, n. 2.

2. C. Bigg, *The Christian Platonists of Alexandria* (1913), p.210.

3. H. Chadwick, *Early Christian Thought and the Classical Tradition*, Clarendon Press, Oxford 1966, p.123.

4. J. B. Mozley, *Baptismal Regeneration*, p. lxii.

5. E. B. Pusey, 'Summary of Objections Against the Proposed Theological Statute' (1854), pp.10, 12.

6. J. Conington, 'The Theological Statute', p. 3.

7. J. W. Burgon, 'Plea for a Fifth Final School' (1868), p.21.

8. H. J. S. Smith, 'The Proposed School of Theology' (Whit Monday 1869).

9. J. W. Burgon, 'To Professor Henry J. S. Smith: The Theological Statute', (18 May 1869). Cited by D. Jenkins, 'Oxford – the Anglican Tradition' in J. Coulson (ed.), *Theology and the University*, Darton, Longman & Todd 1964, p.156.

10. P. E. Pusey (ed.), The Three Epistles of St. Cyril (1872).

11. W. Lock, 'To the Members of the Board of the Faculty of Theology' (14 January 1904), pp.5–6.

12. Appeal to Members of Convocation (May 1904), signed by W. Ince, H. Wace, W. Lock, E. C. S. Gibson, T. B. Strong and R. L. Ottley.

13. 'Theological Degrees at Oxford' (24 March 1913), signed by H. Scott Holland, S. R. Driver, W. Sanday, T. B. Strong, W. Lock, R. Ottley, E. W. Watson and G. A. Cooke.

14. 'Oxford Divinity Degrees and the School of Theology' (31 March 1913).

15. *Letters of the Revd. J. B. Mozley*, p. 190.

16. R. D. Hampden, *The Scholastic Philosophy Considered in Relation to Christian Theology*, p.544.

17. Ibid., pp.376–9.

18. J. B. Mozley, *Lectures and Other Theological Papers*, p.190.

19. *Some Memorials of Renn Dickson Hampden* (edited by his daughter), p.58.

20. R. D. Hampden, Inaugural Lecture, 17 March 1836, p.20.

21. Mozley, *Lectures and Theological Papers*, p.89.

22. Hampden, op. cit., p.186.

23. Mozley, op. cit., p.229.

24. *Letters of the Revd. J. B. Mozley*, p.319.

25. Hampden, op. cit., pp.381, 391.

26. Mozley, op. cit., pp.63, 73.

27. W. Pannenberg, *Basic Questions in Theology*, SCM Press 1970, vol. I, p.6.

28. Published in *Expository Times*, LXXXIII, no. 1, October 1971, pp.4–9.

29. Michael Foster, 'The Christian Doctrine of Creation and the Rise of Natural Science', *Mind*, XLIII, 1934, p.52.

30. W. H. Auden, 'Criticism in a Mass Society', *The Mint*, 2, 1948, p.4; cited by E. R. Dodds, *The Greeks and the Irrational*, University of California Press 1951, pp.237–8.

14. The Criteria of Christian Theology

Theology, LXXVI, December 1973, pp.619–28. Originally read as the presidential paper to the Society for the Study of Theology meeting at Lancaster in April 1973.

1. H. P. Owen, 'Some Philosophical Problems in Christian Ethics', *Theology*, LXXVI, January 1973, pp.15–21.

2. Athanasius, *De Inc.*, 17.

3. D. Cupitt, *Crisis of Moral Authority*, Lutterworth 1972.

INDEX